Summer
versus School

Summer versus School

The Possibilities of the Year-Round School

JAMES M. PEDERSEN

ROWMAN & LITTLEFIELD
Lanham • Boulder • New York • London

Published by Rowman & Littlefield
A wholly owned subsidiary of The Rowman & Littlefield Publishing Group, Inc.
4501 Forbes Boulevard, Suite 200, Lanham, Maryland 20706
www.rowman.com

Unit A, Whitacre Mews, 26-34 Stannary Street, London SE11 4AB

British Library Cataloguing in Publication Information Available

Library of Congress Cataloging-in-Publication Data Available

ISBN 978-1-4758-1254-1 (cloth : alk. paper)
ISBN 978-1-4758-1255-8 (pbk. : alk. paper)
ISBN 978-1-4758-1256-5 (electronic)

♾™ The paper used in this publication meets the minimum requirements of
American National Standard for Information Sciences—Permanence of Paper
for Printed Library Materials, ANSI/NISO Z39.48-1992.

Printed in the United States of America

Contents

PART IV

Preface

BACKGROUND INFORMATION

As I enter into my twentieth year in education I think back to how much has changed over the last several decades from the time I was a student in the public school system—as well as the things that haven't. A myriad of reforms and initiatives have come and gone—like Whole Language and the metric system. Others, though, like standardized tests have actually gained in prominence and increased in frequency as well as weight. But the last couple of years have witnessed a multitude of endeavors that make the No Child Left Behind act seem minor in comparison.

At the time this book is being written, the following are a just a few of the things that are at the forefront of educational reform today.

- Common Core Standards in place in forty-six states across the nation that are changing the way teachers deliver their instruction;
- The new PARCC (Partnership for Assessment of Readiness for Colleges and Careers) that will completely change the way that we assess our students;
- A new evaluation system for teachers, administrators, and superintendents that works on a growth model that may lead to performance pay;
- A vastly competitive job market that differs drastically from when I graduated from college where a bachelor's degree could almost guarantee a job but simply isn't enough in today's economic times;

- Pension reform and a definite downward turn in the perception of teachers and educators that may have a negative effect on the number of people entering the profession within the next several years;
- An increase in the number of charter schools, home schooling, and online learning providers;
- Technological advancements occurring at a seemingly geometric rate that surpass what actually is being used in the classrooms; and
- Proposals across several states and even an endorsement from President Obama to expand education to provide universal pre-k programs across the nation's schools.

In addition to these items there is also a small movement that has also gained momentum over the last few decades—*Year-Round Education.*

Sadly, though, it is not yet at the forefront of educational reforms—at least not exactly.

Indeed, the Common Core Initiative has taken a tremendous amount of traction and appears to be at the top of most of the educational discussions at workshops, in articles, and in online forums. I believe that after the Common Core is fully enmeshed in schools across the country that the assessments created to evaluate these standards in classrooms will show that the amount of time spent on instruction will once again have to be reexamined.

But there are also hints of what the future will bring. President Obama, in addition to governors from several states, has already been firm on universal pre-k, which is going to expand the educational continuum for students; and the PARCC is looking to address postsecondary planning. It is interesting that schools are continuing to be encouraged to add pre-k programs to better prepare students for entering school, but what is missing is addressing the crucial time between the months of June and September. The only area left for improvement is to reevaluate the antiquated school calendar to accommodate the needs of the twenty-first-century student.

Governor Chris Christie from the state of New Jersey during his 2014 State of the State Address included year-round schooling as one of the initiatives that he will be undertaking. Although economics always takes a role in these decisions, it is interesting to see that we are at the precipice of change. Some politicians are beginning to see the merits of calendar reform and improving the public school system to address the needs of the twenty-first-century student.

I firmly believe that the ten-month traditional school calendar will most certainly become a thing of the past.

It is not a matter of *if,* but *when.*

It had occurred to me, even when I was a student myself, that summer vacation served no real academic purpose. Having a teacher for a father meant that he ensured that I worked independently during the months of July and August on all of my subject areas—even when I was in high school. Perhaps that could have been the beginning of my own experience with addressing *Summer Fade*—a topic that will be fully explained later in the book.

This is why when it came time for me to find a dissertation topic when I was completing my doctoral work at Seton Hall University, I decided to research the topic of how year-round high schools performed in comparison to high schools using traditional school calendars.

Surprisingly, the results from my doctoral study found that traditional-calendar high schools actually performed better on standardized tests than their year-round counterparts. I realize that this may seem contrary to the purpose of this book but actually it helped me understand the complexity of year-round education—specifically the challenges that it creates at the secondary level especially when it comes to student achievement.

Having spent a majority of my professional career at the high school level, I was very sensitive to these findings and even predicted that more time does not guarantee increased student performance. I also know that if I had confined my research to just the elementary and middle school levels, my results would have been very different, showing that year-round education has a profound effect on these students.

So what was the big difference that occurs at the high school level?

With all of my experience and insight I knew that I could find the reasons and therefore help people understand that year-round education can be a possibility for everyone. But one of the major obstacles to overcome was the incorrect assumption that year-round schooling could only be achieved by increasing the number of days in the school calendar.

CONSIDERATIONS

My doctoral study enlightened me on the challenges and complexities of implementing a year-round school calendar (Pedersen 2011). More importantly, it made me realize some considerations that arise in the planning and implementation of this type of reform.

- **Space vs. Instruction**—In my study I analyzed year-round high schools in California, Illinois, and Texas. Results showed standardized test scores from these schools were significantly lower than their ten-month peers. One of the limitations of my study was that it only studied schools that labeled themselves as *year-round* and didn't specify for what reason they decided to change their calendars. There are two major reasons schools used year-round calendar—to address overcrowding or for instructional purposes for enhancing learning that includes decreasing the length of the summer break. If a year-round calendar is implemented for space reasons, which most of my high schools in the comparison group were, student achievement will most likely not occur, which is why for the purposes of this book, year-round reform is viewed in the instructional perspective and not for decreasing student population, which in my study did not have any positive impact on student performance and achievement.
- **Grade Levels**—Where this book differs from others regarding calendar reform is that it acknowledges the unique needs of different age groups when implementing year-round calendars as well as the complexities that it involves. When discussing calendar reform there is often an incorrect assumption that all schools from pre-kindergarten to grade twelve must follow the same schedule. Not only is this not true for academic calendars; in most cases around the country it isn't even true for their daily schedules. Bell schedules could be vastly different; early childhood, elementary, middle, and secondary schools can all have different daily schedules even within the same district. Therefore, it is important to provide suggestions that are age and grade sensitive. Too often, the unique needs of the district, region, or state are not taken into consideration. As will be revealed in later chapters, year-round education can look like many different things and be balanced to fit the specific needs of the school and its students.

- **Private, Charter, and Public**—Although most of the information and suggestions contained in this book can be applied for private and charter schools, its design was based on the public education framework. Therefore, many of the anticipated obstacles are based on my experience and research within the public school system. But as the reader will readily see, these challenges can be applied to any educational setting.
- **Longitudinal Studies**—Currently, there are no substantive studies regarding the success of American public school students who have spent their entire pre-kindergarten–twelve experience in a year-round calendar environment. This is due to a variety of reasons—change of district leadership, funding, and other issues. For example, some districts may have elementary schools with year-round calendars while their high schools don't. In other cases, schools may start with year-round calendars but will discontinue their use for several reasons that include financial or lack of administrative support.

PURPOSE

The intent of this book is to provide readers the opportunity to envision how year-round schools could be implemented in our country. Hopefully, the reader will be persuaded that year-round education is not just some fad but an inevitability that only needs to have a roadmap for its execution. Just as kindergarten, pre-k, and college were once reserved for a small segment of the American population several decades ago, so too will year-round education become as seemingly omnipresent.

For supporters of year-round schools what will be found in this book will be examples and suggestions for how to implement balanced calendars across the country. They are presented generally, but hopefully provide educators with enough material so that they can be applied to the needs of almost any type of school in any part of the country.

For the opposition, the information contained will give those readers enough impetus to reconsider their stance. The suggestions and the recommendations in the book are meant to spawn additional discussions and arguments as to the best way year-round schools can be implemented.

The aim of this manuscript, in addition to providing a background on the history of how summer vacation became part of the educational paradigm, will be to create an argument for the reexamination of how students spend their summer vacations. This redesign of the school calendar at first can sound a bit frightening, but upon closer examination it can address such issues as

- Decreasing the achievement gap by assisting at-risk and struggling students who could benefit with a consistent instructional calendar;
- Providing opportunities for additional courses in the humanities, math, science, and engineering fields;
- Establishing opportunities for students to participate in community service;
- Pursuing the arts and humanities electives that are often marginalized during the regular year;
- Increasing participation in new and innovative programs;
- Enrolling in online learning classes;
- Participating in college-level classes; and
- Allowing students to enroll in internship and job shadowing experiences.

Optimistically, I would hope that this book could be embraced as a blueprint to implementing year-round schools across the United States. But I would be very content knowing that the research and ideas contained herein may be the impetus for the beginnings of change that will inevitably end with year-round education across the country.

In looking ahead toward the future, embracing a calendar that more closely resembles the learners that we want to cultivate—who learn consistently, without six to eight weeks of breaks interrupting them, will be the rule instead of the exception.

As American educational reformers continue to find innovative ways to address the global achievement gap, many experts seem to agree that increasing instructional time is a viable option. In addition to extending the school day, some educational leaders have looked to modifying the traditional academic calendar to address some of the academic losses that occur when students have eight to ten weeks of summer vacation each year. Reexamining how students spend their summer vacation, although considered by many to be a cultural taboo, may be the answer to addressing global competition and decreasing the national achievement gap.

The need for a two-month break from schools harkens back to a pre-industrial time that no longer is pertinent for our students. Although an answer may be staring us in the face, are we willing to give up on the American tradition of summer vacation all in the name of reform and student success?

Summer versus School offers a historical perspective of how summer vacation became so enmeshed in American culture and provides ideas of what a future without a two-and-a-half-month break could possibly look like. Is it possible that parents, educators, and leaders have been overlooking the most obvious opportunity of two months of schooling all along? After all, in the century and a half of research, no study has ever produced the need for an extensive summer break to increase student achievement.

ORGANIZATION OF THE BOOK

This book is organized into four parts to better provide the reader with the background, examples, and suggestions for the implementation of year-round school calendars.

Part I provides information pertinent to understanding the history of how summer vacations were implemented in the American school system. This overview is intended to be in-depth for those already familiar with the subject but not so dense for newcomers of calendar reform. Part I also explores the actual need for year-round education. This portion of the book also summarizes the many proponents and opponents of year-round schooling, providing perspective from both camps to better illustrate the many challenges this reform faces in becoming fully embraced.

Part II examines year-round schools within America and across the world. These comparisons provide the reader with a broader sense of how different schools manage their academic calendars, which operate free from the traditional confines of their American counterparts. As the U.S. educational program is constantly being compared using international standards, it is important that the calendars from these schools be described.

Part III proposes some examples of what year-round schools would look like in the United States. The chapters are broken up into various grades so that more customized and age-appropriate suggestions are made. These chapters are intended as suggestions and templates for readers to conceptualize year-round schooling.

Finally, Part IV looks toward the future and how year-round education would impact the various educational stakeholders to illustrate how each group could be positively impacted by this paradigm shift. This section attempts to predict and anticipate some of the next steps as the nation moves toward year-round learning.

Acknowledgments

This book is dedicated to my family—my wife, Faith, and our three daughters, Emily, Veronica, and Cynthia; my parents, Regina and Neil; my sister, Jenifer; and my step-parents, Rosemary and Dennis. They have always been supportive in my educational and professional endeavors and have provided the stability necessary for me to accomplish the many goals that I have set. Whether they realize it or not, each of them has played a crucial role in my success and for that I am deeply grateful and appreciative.

I would like to acknowledge my fellow cohort members from my doctorate program at Seton Hall University—Lucky Cohort 13. Although it has been several years since I graduated, the seeds for this book were planted during my studies at that time. I entered the program being fascinated with the possibilities of year-round schooling and tried my best to turn every discussion that I could back onto that topic. My fellow students were always supportive and continue to be my friends, both professionally and personally, over these last few years.

I would like to very much thank my staff at South Plainfield High School in South Plainfield, N.J. I took every opportunity to engage my colleagues in the discourse of year-round education. Some agreed, some argued, and others were outraged. But our discussions were always spirited and their expertise and experience were crucial because it helped me anticipate arguments and question some of my own thoughts in preparation for this book. My assistant principals, Joe, Kelly, and Ron, were always considerate of my passion and would allow me to bring up the topic of changing school calendars quite often. My secretary, Teri, is truly a blessing and manages to keep me organized. I am very privileged to be surrounded by a group of intelligent people.

I would also like to thank my editor and assistant editor at Rowman & Littlefield, Tom Koerner and Carlie Wall. This is my second book with this company and I am very appreciative to be working with such professionals. They are both very responsive and attentive—which makes the production side of writing much easier for a writer.

Lastly, I would like to acknowledge all of the pioneers of year-round education who have already adopted balanced calendars and are at the forefront of educational reform—especially Charles Ballinger and Carolyn Kneese as well as the research and meta-analyses completed by Harris Cooper. In conducting research for my doctoral studies and this book, Cooper, Valentine, Charlton, and Barnett have led the way in examining calendar reform.

In several decades we will all find ourselves looking back at our school calendars from the early twenty-first century as a remnant from the previous two centuries. The balanced calendars currently in use will be seen as trailblazers. In the very near future year-round calendars will be ubiquitous as soon as it becomes apparent to all stakeholders that learning doesn't have a vacation and that American students deserve an opportunity to expand their knowledge and better prepare themselves to compete with their international peers.

I

Summer and the American School System

The History of Summer Vacation

The history of summer vacation and the American educational system is a little more complex than most people may think. In fact, one would venture that not much time at all is devoted to thinking about summer vacation—unless it relates directly to how it will be spent vacationing away from school. But what makes this issue truly perplexing is why a centuries-old working school calendar persists in the new millennium and why, to a great extent, it has remained consistently unaddressed by parents, educational leaders, politicians, and other stakeholders.

After all, there is little, if any, pertinent research that even begins to suggest that an eight-to-ten-week vacation optimizes student learning or that summer vacations improve academic performance and benefit cognitive development in school-age children. Yet, as a nation we continue to ignore the possibilities that could exist by reimagining the way we create our school calendars while other countries that have embraced the concept and are implementing year-round schools for their children are seeing some great strides in their overall improvement. In all other aspects of working life in the United States, there are very few examples of jobs that have ten weeks of continuous breaks on an annual basis.

It is quite common to hear that educators prepare their children for the workforce. In fact, the metaphor given to children is that school is their job. Both have many similarities, including commutes, lunch breaks, and structure. But this comparison becomes less relevant when looking at their calendars.

In the workplace, common vacations, including holidays, range from four to six weeks. In the public school system it can range from ten to twelve weeks, including holidays. Therefore, schools with traditional calendars are not the ideal comparison to what life will be like as a full-time worker.

WHY DO WE EVEN HAVE A SUMMER VACATION?

When asked what is the history of summer vacation, most will respond that it originally had something to do with the agrarian calendar and the need for children to tend to the fields to help their parents during the harvest seasons.

In our country's past, children were often viewed as cheap labor and were integral to farming communities as a means to manage the crops that were central to their survival. For many families, their very livelihood depended on the assistance of their children during the crucial harvesting season; even though education was important, their survival took precedence over school at that time in our country's history.

Children were viewed much differently than they are today. Few, if any, rights were given to them. Legislative reform, which vastly improved conditions and began to set safety requirements and age restrictions, did not take place until the beginning of the nineteenth century, which saw the beginnings of mandatory schooling laws in the states. Not surprisingly, this period also saw a positive change in compulsory school attendance and other laws that positively impacted children.

Although there is some truth to the need for children to work on farms, it only really affected a small population of children and still doesn't sufficiently explain why, as our country expanded and child welfare laws became stricter with each succeeding generation, states across the country continued using this type of antiquated calendar. What some may also find surprising is that in the early twentieth century certain districts, especially urban ones like Newark, New Jersey, used calendars that extended well into the summer months (Pedersen 2012).

Other, more recent, responses to why summer vacations were necessary in the past would most likely point to the fact that many schools still aren't equipped with the proper air conditioning that would allow for the appropriate learning environment needed for instruction. School buildings, especially the older ones, are not conducive for instructional purposes. On this, most people would likely agree.

Because of this, this point has merit and should be taken into serious consideration. In many places across the country the temperatures during the summer months can be unbearably hot and schools are still without the appropriate climate control abilities due to costs, antiquated structures, and other challenges. Although I started my career working summer school in buildings without air conditioning, students and teachers alike are much more sensitive to working under these conditions today than they were twenty years ago. Increases in student health issues like asthma and diabetes also are of great concern during normal temperatures, never mind the hot and uncomfortably warm months of July and August when temperatures can soar above 100° and place students in harm's way.

But as schools continued to be built in the United States and have been periodically updated over the last few decades, this reason is becoming less and less relevant. In fact, most municipalities even require that all newer buildings, especially schools, be equipped with air conditioning so that temperatures can be regulated even during the more mild seasons. This is most obvious in the southern states that are prone to extremely warm summers. But in some states, like Nevada for example, air conditioning has been a standard practice for the last fifty years or more.

SO WHAT IS THE PROBLEM?

So if farming and air conditioning are no longer the obstacles that they once were, what is then actually getting in the way of changing the school calendar to a year-round one?

Is it political?

Does it have something to do with money and economics?

Is it about resources like buildings and staffing?

Is it about the teacher unions and contracts?

Or is summer vacation just part of the fabric of our country's culture? Is it, as some say, the last true remaining common thread of the American culture that is able to keep us together and far more important than year-round schooling?

Each one of these questions and their responses play a role in the reason why, for the most part, calendar reform remains one of the topics that requires the most attention and sometimes provides as much opposition as it does support.

What adults don't look back fondly on the many memories they have of their own summer vacations? After all, it seems that everyone can remember times from childhood and fondly look back at those lazy days of summer—when children played outside until the streetlights came on and every day felt like a Saturday morning. There were places to go to, relatives to visit, and barbeques to be had.

Last, what could never be forgotten is the time-honored tradition of the family vacation—the one time in which families would get together to go camping, visit Disney World, see relatives, or vacation at the beach or in the country. These experiences strengthen familial bonds and are an important part of being in a family.

Aren't these things important enough to keep summer vacations the way they are?

Are these enough reasons to leave summer vacation out of the hands of educational reformers?

Perhaps approaching year-round education isn't what people may expect. Does year-round school have to take away all, or any, of those things that are held so precious in the American consciousness?

Not necessarily.

Although some schools may utilize a balanced calendar or extended calendar, other schools implement an intersession that takes place during the summer that could easily accommodate time for family vacations and summer retreats as well as academic enrichment and extended learning that may not be cost prohibitive (Ballinger 1998).

Most importantly, what would more time in school look like and would it really make a difference? There have been dozens of programs over the last few decades that have extended the school day or added Saturdays; has there been any real success with more time? Perhaps this may be the greatest challenge—the fear of the unknown.

Ironically, it's not all that scary, nor is it all that unknown. The next few chapters will reveal the successes, failures, and new ideas that will help year-round education become part of the American fabric.

Year-round schools and summer intersession-like programs that will be explained in later chapters have been in existence for decades and can be used as a template for calendar reform. As a matter of fact, in the future, one may even view these programs as the first steps to nationwide calendar reform that resulted in universal year-round education in our country.

HISTORICAL PERSPECTIVE

Summer vacation wasn't widely instituted until the late nineteenth century. It was during this time when one of the measurements of a good school had been the number of days it was open (Weiss and Brown 2005). Therefore, better schools were perceived by many professionals at the time to be open longer during the year than their counterparts.

In fact, it was really the financial state of the district that determined how long the school was open during the year. Although schools with longer calendars were often accepted by the general public as more effective, many districts were not able to shoulder the financial obligations it took to run these types of schools. Until educational reforms in the last century sought to unify schools, many districts operated on a calendar that varied from region to region based on the unique needs of the community (Weiss and Brown 2003). The calendar of an urban school in the east could look very different from one in the west.

The nine-month calendar that is used in the majority of American schools today was never initially intended to be the standard calendar for schools (Ballinger and Kneese 2006). If anything, the current calendar was a compromise of the existing school calendars of the time from schools around a particular region. The goal, of course, was uniformity rather than any real sound pedagogical decision that would increase academic achievement or address any other student needs.

This is probably when the idea of the traditional summer vacation seemed to have become part of the fabric of American culture that has spanned over the course of the last two hundred years.

Currently, the summer holiday is viewed by many Americans as the backbone of our country's school system (Weiss and Brown 2003). In addition, the revenues of many seasonal industries have become dependent on the openings and closings of the traditional school calendar. Summer-themed attractions for children seem to give credence to the metaphor given by one writer that the school schedule is one of the "great clocks of our society" (Weiss and Brown 2003).

But questions regarding the efficacy of summer vacation can be seen in the early twentieth century. Some educators were wary of how many children returned to school in September unprepared or behind in their academics. For the past 100 years researchers have begun to document what has been referred to as summer fade or *summer slide* as the decline in student achievement that occurs during the time when summer break begins and school begins (Borman and Dowling 2006).

As early as 1684, a grammar school founded in Massachusetts required twelve months of education. Most students attended school eleven or twelve months a year beginning in the 1840s (Ballinger and Kneese 2006). In 1841, Boston schools operated for 244 days while Philadelphia implemented a 251-day calendar (Association of California School Administrators 1988). According to Silva, at the beginning of the nineteenth century, large cities commonly had long school years, ranging from 251 to 260 days (2007). During this time, many of these rural schools were only open about six months out of the year. Glines first wrote that the origin for the traditional school calendar based purely on agrarian needs was not entirely accurate (1995). In the nineteenth century districts organized their calendars around the needs of the community with most of the country's population residing in rural areas.

For example, some special provisions were made for vacations during September and October for communities with large fall harvests. Prior to 1890, students in major urban areas were in school for eleven months a year. But by 1900, the more popular 180-day, nine-month calendar had been firmly established. Year-round programs were implemented in such places as Bluffton, Indiana (1904), Newark, New Jersey (1912), Aliquippa (1928) and Ambridge (1931) Pennsylvania, Nashville, Tennessee (1925), Omaha, Nebraska (1924), and Minot, North Dakota (Glines 1997).

Many twelve-month schools called for a two-week vacation during the summer, which was then extended to four weeks. The reasons for the increase were attributed to high absenteeism due to hot and unhealthy summer months; epidemics, vacations, and general truancy of students were other contributing factors. Some urban centers in America such as Buffalo, Detroit, and Philadelphia changed from year-round in the middle part of the century to a two-month holiday by the late nineteenth century. In rural areas the dates would change depending on funding problems, fuel, harvest, and the weather conditions (Weiss and Brown 2003).

Year-round schooling was also used in some areas across the country to address rapid population growth. It wasn't until 1968–1970 that year-round education was established in Missouri, Illinois, California, and Minnesota to have students attend school the entire calendar year to accommodate the increasing student population (Glines 1997).

A majority of districts that adopted year-round schools during 1970–1990 did so to maximize space (Hazleton 1992). In 1972, California seemed to lead the way in the resurgence of year-round calendars, creating the first multi-track calendar schools in La Mesa, Spring Valley, and Chula Vista to address large increases in student enrollment (Ballinger and Kneese 2006). These schools were created to address the overwhelming increase in school populations. Some people may also know this as *split-sessions*. Also in that same year, educators from existing year-round schools formed the National Association for Year-Round Education (NAYRE 2014).

Most recently, year-round schools have also become popular in different settings such as charter schools. In these cases, the charters use this as an advantage to attract more students to attend their schools. This occurs most often at the early childhood and elementary levels but can also be found at the later grades as well.

The popularity in public schools, though, has been inconsistent and fraught with challenges from the economic downturn causing a sharp decrease in the size of school budgets. In some situations, schools that had twelve-month schedules had to move back to a traditional calendar to reduce spending. Schools addressing overcrowding, however, still adopted year-round calendars as a financial tactic to reduce costs and prepare for potential new construction.

SUMMARY

Unfortunately, there had always been two great barriers that made it difficult for schools to be in session for the entire year—the vestiges of the agrarian calendar and the limitations of the building facilities themselves. But as the need for the agrarian calendar has been removed, the need for a two-and-a-half-month vacation seems, at the very least, antiquated. With American students expected to compete in the global arena it is imperative that districts seek to find ways to increase instructional time and decrease the amount of time students spend not formally engaged in learning. With the ever-increasing demands of the economic landscape it is important that we prepare students from the very early grades to master skills that are competitive with their international peers. Understanding the reasons that year-round calendars aren't already in place throughout the country is almost as important as the reasons calendar reform is necessary.

2

Calendars and Vacations

How Americans Spend Their Time

SCHOOL CALENDARS

Currently in America, most school calendars average approximately 180 days with some small breaks during the year and a summer vacation that could last anywhere from eight to ten weeks. In comparison, several studies have reported that nations with more than 180 instructional days and have calendars that are year-round have outperformed American schools (Farbman and Kaplan 2005). Some public, private, and charter schools in the United States have responded to this educational dilemma by taking steps to extend their school days or their school year in order to boost student achievement (Neal 2008).

In 2010, close to two million students in the United States followed some form of a balanced schedule (Huebner 2010). Many of these schools were "designated" year-round and still operated in the same districts with other schools that followed traditional calendars. Other programs sought to increase instructional time in other ways that were created to address their own specific needs.

BREAKING AWAY FROM THE PACK

For example, many of these schools offered after-school classes that extended the school day beyond their usual dismissal time. These extended days would include additional instruction, remediation, or other elective classes for the students. Schools have been very creative in exploring the many ways of providing additional times or days for their students and have realized that with the right support, time can be manipulated to fit the needs of the school. In some cases they may provide short-term solutions that address such things as preparing for standardized exams; or they could be after-care programs for younger children that supplement the instructional program.

In much the same manner, morning programs would also be implemented to provide additional classes that would supplement instruction. In many schools across the nation, state educational mandates require a full complement of courses that create scheduling challenges that make it difficult for students to take elective and advanced courses.

Last, some even opened up on Saturdays, exploring a six-day school week that may have looked exactly like some of their international peers; the intent was usually to provide academic interventions to improve student performance.

ACADEMIC PERFORMANCE

Although these schools displayed varying degrees of success, most districts embraced the concept of year-round education as a more comprehensive means to increasing academic achievement. As the emphasis on standardized test scores has become a major impetus for reform, districts sought a systemic change that would hopefully improve productivity with their students (Aronson 1995). These schools adopted new calendars that differed greatly from the traditional ten-month one that students and teachers had been used to using.

It is also important to note that funding in most districts across the country depends on student performance scores and whether it is national encouragement, such as No Child Left Behind, or state-led initiatives, school systems have felt the pressure to improve underperforming schools.

In *School Calendar Reform: Learning in All Seasons*, Ballinger and Kneese (2006) explain that the traditional calendar is indeed not a learning calendar designed for instructional purposes. The traditional ten months is not the most effective means to instructing students in a fluid and consistent manner. A change is needed to provide students and teachers the opportunity to learn in a much more natural state. They further go on to stress that flexibility, not rigidity, is the first step to addressing the needs of the students. It is important that educators understand that only through reexamining the use of time, in a vastly different way than we are used to, can schools begin to develop new constructs that will benefit their own communities.

Breaking away from the educational canon is the only way that reformers can bring schools to the next level of progress.

The types of calendars and number of days vary depending on the needs of the particular school or district. For example, a multitrack calendar can accommodate large student populations and may address certain fiscal restraints while an extended year would add more instructional time with the goal of improving student achievement.

NONTRADITIONAL CALENDARS

There is a variety of types of nontraditional calendars currently in use across the country. What follows is a brief overview of the various models that some districts employ to address calendar reform.

- **Balanced 45/15 Single-Track Calendar**: This calendar has forty-five days of instruction and fifteen days of break across the entire calendar year. The school year usually begins in September and ends in early August.
- **Balanced 60/20 Calendar**: This model divides the school year into trimesters with sixty days of instruction followed by twenty days of breaks across the calendar year. This model can also begin in September and end in August.
- **Balanced 90/30 Calendar**: In this example, the school uses ninety days of instruction followed by thirty days of vacation with a September start as well.
- **Extended year**: This is a blanket term used for any calendar that goes beyond the traditional 180 days of instruction. In some cases, this can be as much as 200 days.
- **Intersessions**: This model more closely resembles how colleges implement their two condensed semesters during the two months of July and August. Each intersession has a condensed schedule that runs three to four weeks and can also be divided into morning and afternoon sessions.
- **Summer Based Learning Labs (SBLL)**: SBLL schools would continue to use the traditional 180-day calendar but would then supplement the summer months with several short three-to-four-week classes used for project-based learning and field trips.

- **Cyber-Summer School**: In this newer addition to year-round schooling, schools use the traditional 180-day calendar and then supplement with a variety of activities and software that can be completed online. In some ways, this can be viewed as the modern equivalent of the summer reading list used in previous generations.

SUMMER VACATIONS TODAY

Since very few American students today have the same farming obligations as their predecessors from over a century ago and most buildings constructed in the past twenty years are equipped with the necessary climate control, the original obstacles for year-round education, for the most part, seem to have been removed as a scheduling barrier for public schools.

Yet, this is not the case for the majority of American schools who continue to operate for only ten months out of the calendar year in spite of the antiquated nature of this design. Some research suggests that fewer than half of the students in America are engaged in some sort of summer program and although that is a significant number, there is still a great deal of work that remains in convincing those other districts (Ballinger and Kneese 2006).

THE DEFICITS

The deficits that occur from *summer fade*, a term that refers to the time between the ending of school and its beginning, when many students do not receive any formal education, most often severely impact students from low socioeconomic areas and at-risk students the hardest. Some studies even claim that as much as three months of academic setback can occur per grade level, negatively impacting student achievement (Cooper et al. 1996).

Other research has found that children from various socioeconomic backgrounds may make similar gains during the school year as their other peers, but those from low socioeconomic groups create academic deficits during their summer months (Cooper et al. 1996; Edmonds et al. 2008; Zuckerbrod 2007).

Last, additional studies have shown that in the last few decades our high-achieving students in America have been steadily losing their educational ranking in the world and spend considerably less instructional time than other countries (Bracey 2002b). High-achieving students are known to benefit from schools with year-round calendars with accelerated programs and advanced classes (Coalition 2009).

TRADITION VERSUS RESEARCH

The traditional school calendar has governed how families organize their lives for well over a century in this country (Rasmussen 2000). Yet, in spite of this tradition there is some growing evidence to suggest that year-round schools are increasing in number among the states (Weiss and Brown 2003). The National Association for Year-Round Education reports that approximately 3,000 schools within 400 school systems in 46 states currently utilize some form of year-round education (2014).

A considerable amount of literature suggests that year-round schools are effective at the earlier grades. Research studies conducted by Alcorn (1992), Downey, von Hippel, and Broh (2004), Edmonds et al. (2008), and McMillen (2001), have all shown that year-round calendars appear to academically benefit elementary and middle school students. Additionally, the meta-analyses of Cooper, Nye, Charlton, Lindsey, and Greathouse (1996), Cooper, Charlton, Valentine, and Muhlenbruck (2000), and Worten and Zsiray (1994) have all supported these findings with over 100 years of studies that have focused primarily on the pre-secondary students (Burkham et al. 2004).

Other researchers have found that lengthening the school year has no immediate impact on student achievement (Ubben 2001). Penta concluded that gains in year-round schools were nullified when racial and socioeconomic variables were taken into consideration and also found that the gains were eventually erased over time (2001). Even Cooper, Nye, Charlton, Lindsey, and Greathouse, whose meta-analysis found gains in student performance, indicated that further research was needed for any serious decisions to be made regarding this topic (1996). Last, some researchers are also skeptical that more time will increase student performance at all and school districts have conducted their own investigations into the success of their year-round programs and have discontinued them for a variety of reasons (Cuban 2008).

For example, the San Diego Unified School District conducted its own study in 1991, where balanced-calendar schools were implemented in 1972 and found no significant difference in student achievement (Wildman et al. 1999). The Alabama school district also returned to a traditional school calendar after several years with year-round schools (Zuckerbrod 2007).

There are over 2,500 year-round schools in the United States with balanced calendars (NAYRE 2014). These schools are comprised of public, private, and charter schools at the elementary, middle, and secondary levels and represent most of the geographical regions in the United States. As more and more schools implement balanced school calendars for all students, it is vital that researchers look at the performance results of all grade levels to determine if year-round education is effective as well as if it is necessary to be implemented for all grade levels in the future.

The year-round calendar affords younger students the ability to continue their education uninterrupted and address key learning areas. At the middle school level, year-round education has been used to address the learning needs of the students as they prepare to enter high school.

Indeed, most of the research that has been conducted regarding year-round education has targeted these two student populations. But the results of this study do not support that gains are made at the high school level. In fact, some of the unplanned and supplementary analyses show that year-round high school students actually had lower passing rates than their traditional peers on standardized tests.

In most cases, year-round calendars at the secondary level are implemented to ease overcrowding issues and seldom for academic achievement. The exceptions of course would be for summer-school remediation, elective courses, and advanced classes, which are all initiatives that are steps to year-round education. Unfortunately, these are usually based on an individual need and lack a cohesive and unifying plan of addressing ways to increase learning during the ten-week summer vacation.

Last, it must also be noted that there are competing priorities regarding the proponents of year-round schools who claim that this model has academic benefits and those who oppose this type of reform.

Many critics of year-round schools argue that summer industries, such as tourism, that tend to utilize student workers, would be greatly affected. Others feel that nonacademic influences such as athletics and family vacations are obstacles that prevent calendar reform in many districts. These societal influences tend to have greater impact in determining if a school will move to a year-round schedule than do the potential academic benefits.

The region of the country is also an important variable to consider. In some places, summer industries are crucial to the local economy and tend to be a very serious consideration. In parts of the country that experience extreme temperatures, experimenting with time has been in place for decades, pioneering calendar reform.

GLOBAL INFLUENCE

American public schools face many challenges today as they try to compete in the global market. In consistent studies American schools continuously fall far behind many other developed countries such as China, Japan, and the Netherlands when it comes to student achievement. Reformers have been scrambling to try new initiatives to address this great educational chasm by developing ways to improve academic achievement (OECD 2009).

In order to prepare adequately for global competition, many districts have begun to rethink how they spend their summer vacations as a means to improve student performance. Educators have also begun to question the value of having students take a ten-to-twelve-week break during the summer months. This break in instruction in no way is perceived by any professional to increase student achievement, and by many is to blame for the less-than-satisfactory academic standing of the American school system.

Countless reports have shown that American schools are not on par with many other countries around the world (Chappel 2013). Measures such as PISA (Programme for International Student Assessment), TIMMS (Trends in Math and Science Study), and others all point to other countries leading the way in student achievement.

The tests used for these comparisons are not without criticism, of course. Certain countries, like China, for example, only use the results from major cities and do not use the entire national average for their reporting. Others cite that if American students prepared for thesis assessments, much like they do with the SAT (Scholastic Aptitude Test), the results would show much more favorable results for the United States.

Regardless of these factors, most Americans are still not satisfied with these rankings and would agree that education, although usually in a constant state of reform, must keep up with the times and find new ways to succeed.

THE FORMER BARRIERS

Besides, with newer climate-controlled school buildings and the lack of child labor needed for farming, the agrarian school calendar leaves many professionals questioning the usefulness of the extended summer vacation that was based on the needs of a pre-Industrial American society.

Are we keeping the calendar simply because we've always done it that way?

Are we afraid of changing what we know in fear of our calendars looking different from what we were used to?

These former barriers are no longer the challenges that they used to be. If the traditional calendar persists is this only because we are too complacent?

And once all of the barriers are removed in the very near future, when all schools are climate controlled and the economy has improved, what will be the reasoning then why schools still operate on an antiquated schedule?

MAKING IT PERSONAL

As we continue to make progress with year-round schools at the elementary and middle school levels, careful attention should also be paid to whether the same types of calendars should be implemented at the high school level as an effective means of educational reform to improve student achievement. This concept is also true for calendar reform in the general sense as well. What works for one school may not be the most effective model for another school even within the same district.

Although coordination is extremely important at schools within the same district to avoid confusion and continue to provide necessary standardization, another important factor is to ensure that the approach to addressing calendar reform works for the school itself. It is extremely important that the personalization of the school be kept in mind when selecting the right type of calendar reform. This should be done with as many stakeholders as possible to achieve the sufficient level of support needed to ensure success with this endeavor.

Ideally, schools should complete the selection, adoption, and implementation of their new calendars independently of other schools, but realistically this may not be possible in many regards. Districts will want to keep the needs of the entire community in mind when making these decisions, which means that when implementing their new calendar a holistic approach to planning may be required.

The later chapters will explore how some of these calendars can be implemented as well as the planning that is involved in the process.

SUMMARY

For more than 100 years the public school system has been the foundation of our society. Millions of our nation's citizens have moved through the primary, middle, and secondary schools which, although they vary slightly from region to region, provided a shared experience and are a part of Americana. History tells us the reasons that school systems only used a ten-month calendar were due to agrarian needs, but in recent years this rationale seems less applicable. In light of global competition and America's consistently poor international rankings, it would seem like a logical conclusion to extend the school year to increase instructional time. But the move to year-round schooling isn't so easy, nor is it unanimously embraced by parents, community members, businesses, or politicians.

The Challenges
to Seeking Reform

The Opponents and the Proponents

OPPONENTS OF YEAR-ROUND EDUCATION

There are a variety of reasons that year-round education is still not readily embraced by many school districts around the country. But hesitancy and apprehension could be true of any type of reform, regardless of whether it was education or in any other field or profession. There tend to always be pockets of resistance that make moving ahead difficult under any circumstances.

In some instances these apprehensions can be based purely on unrealistic fears and exaggerated imaginations, while in other cases they can be based on much more tangible things like reason and experience. But in the discussion of calendar reform, the fears and apprehensions could be much allayed by looking to examples of schools that employ year-round schooling that have succeeded in increasing student engagement and achievement.

Although there are many arguments that are presented by critics of year-round educations, most opponents to year-round education can be placed into one of these several broad categories:

- Those individuals who feel that an extended school year will not increase student achievement and that more time will not make any difference. These critics tend to be skeptical about the merits that additional time will increase student performance.

- A contingent, usually very vocal, who believe in the sanctity of summer vacation as a time for families to tend to vacations, visiting relatives, and other things that are far too important to give up. They believe in the value of the time that is provided during the summer and fear that denying this would negatively impact families and the quality time they have. Summer Matters is one group in particular that has created their own crusade defending the sanctity of summer vacation. Although they would oppose much of what is contained in this book, there are still a few models that they would be pressed to provide any substantial argument.
- Critics who are connected to businesses that thrive on summer business, such as resorts, amusement parks, and other vacation-related services that would be severely affected if students remained in school for most or all of the summer months. In some instances, this could impact their workforce because teenagers might not be able to work during the day. In other cases, business owners are fearful that having more children in school during the summer would decrease profits and sales.
- Conversely, teenagers who rely on summer employment and may be restricted due to extended-year calendars that would require them in school during July and August.
- Taxpayers from the community who believe that an extended year would increase their property taxes. They view additional time as supplemental to the education program and not financially prudent in these economic times.
- Summer camps, Bible schools, and other programs that could be affected by year-round schooling with possible decreases in enrollment. These organizations usually are not supportive of calendar reform and view their services as programs that already address summer learning and enrichment.

THE OBSTACLES

This is not to say that these obstacles aren't very real and extremely challenging. Indeed, there are many things that must be taken into consideration in planning for a school or district to adjust its calendar. As with any type of reform, a great deal of understanding, planning, and executing must be done with sensitivity and coordination.

For example, listed below are only a few of the anticipated arguments that opponents will cite as criticism of calendar reform.

- The **philosophical shift** necessary from viewing summer vacations by many as an American right that can never be touched or modified could be one of the hardest obstacles to overcome. Much in the same way that pre-k has affected education, so too will year-round schools. Not more than thirty years ago many parents still needed convincing that even kindergarten was necessary, never mind pre-kindergarten for their children. As previously stated, there currently is a push for universal pre-k because of the benefits it has on student development as well as early intervention. Although it would have been scoffed at thirty years ago, universal pre-k has become a growing topic that will also become a reality within our lifetime. During my own experience, I have witnessed the perception of pre-kindergarten being synonymous with day care change to an instructionally sound program where academics, socialization, and early intervention are employed. The requirements for the instructors have changed as well with today's teachers required to pass tests with at least a bachelor's degree.

- **More time** does not bring about student achievement. In fact, doing more the same of anything would most definitely only serve to increase frustration—not to mention teacher and student burnout. Additional time must be spent wisely and constructively. This could look very different from what is currently being implemented in schools across the country and could look like schools in other countries or be completely different. One of the major stigmas associated with having school during the summer is that it is associated with remediation. When most people think of summer school they think of students who have to attend classes that they have failed already. This negative association leads to the negative attitude that many people have with instituting year-round education. Another one of the biggest obstacles to overcome is to assure stakeholders that year-round calendars, especially the intersessions, are not going to be more of the same or used just for remediation. The emphasis is on exploring new ways to engage students and preparing them for their future through innovative programs that cannot really be accomplished during the traditional school year.

- **Teacher unions** could also present some resistance to year-round implementation if they are brought into the planning process. If school calendars redistribute time, then additional salary increases will not be necessary. But if teachers are working additional days beyond their previous contractual agreements, their salaries would undoubtedly have to increase. It is important to reiterate that additional school days is only one of several suggestions to address calendar reform and is most likely the most costly. When looking for a type of calendar model that fits the needs of the school or district, it is important to note the financial limitations because this will impact the decision-making process.

- **Professional Development** is vital for any type of year-round education model. Teachers will need to be prepared to involve a variety of teaching strategies that will engage students and keep their attention. The costs for professional development could vary greatly. In some instances, certain instructional strategy workshops could be presented by teachers within the district, saving considerable costs. In other cases, districts might employ high-level presenters that could be very costly.

- **Teacher/administrator/staff burnout** is also a serious consideration (Gismodi 2005) in modifying traditional school calendars. Ideally buy-in and shared vision will be necessary for such changes but sometimes this could be not so easy. There are dozens of examples of districts in the United States that have changed their calendars without support, and sometimes even knowledge, of their stakeholders. In most of these examples the results are uneven at best. Getting 100 percent buy-in might not be possible, but increasing the percentage is advantageous to successful implementation.

- Without **parent buy-in** the initiative will not be able to succeed (Gismodi 2005). When parents realize the money that is spent on summer day care they will very quickly see the benefits to a balanced school calendar. Parents need only look to the amount of money and time they already spend to attend to their children during the months of summer to understand that reform is necessary. Summer camps, day camps, and other programs were all created, and thrived, because of the gap that public schools created during the months of June, July, and August (depending on the traditional calendar used, some student can get out of school as early as the first week of June).

- **Student buy-in** may not seem like a possibility at first, but if students are able to be convinced of the value and new programs that they could participate in, their support could be easily gained. The most convincing will be needed at the middle and high school grades where students have begun to exercise their independence. But if these students can participate in things that can prepare them for their colleges and careers, their support could be easily attained.

- Year-round schools with extended days may impact **sports and extra-curricular activities** if a balanced calendar is not used. For example, breaks may occur during certain seasons that would prevent them from having a sufficient number of games to qualify for participation in county and state tournaments. When considering that athletic programs, especially at the high school level, play an important role in college admissions and scholarships, this challenge must be given the sufficient amount of attention to ensure that students do not suffer because of the adopted model. This is one of several reasons that intersessions and other models that would not interfere with athletic programs would work much better at the middle and high school levels. Intersessions and Summer Based Learning Labs (SBLL) allow for flexibility and ease that are required for students at these ages as they also learn to handle other commitments in their lives like family, work, and socialization.
- **Family vacations** may need to be rescheduled, and this could present some difficulties when families plan large get-togethers with children who have different school calendars. Vacation schedules will not always match their children's and this could be a problem for some families who need or have to take their holidays at specific times of the year for reasons that could have to do with time-sharing resorts and hotels, prescheduled family gatherings and reunions, work-related peak and off-peak allotted vacation times, and other such issues (Ballinger and Kneese 2006).
- **Financial increases** such as materials, teacher pay, electricity, and other expenses could necessitate tax increases that would not be looked upon favorably by most community members depending on the model that the school, district, or state adopts. As the nation is still recovering from its economic crisis, many citizens are not looking for additional ways to spend their money on reform that some may consider supplemental. In my experience, though, if people waited for the right financial time to implement new programs little, if any, reform would ever be implemented. The economic situations of districts must be considered in determining the type of calendar reform but should not be the only obstacle that cannot be overcome. As will be explained in later chapters, a variety of initiatives could be implemented that increase student achievement and summer learning can be used and expanded upon. For example, school can begin with programs aimed at grades pre-kindergarten though first grade for the first year and

then expand to include second through fourth grades in the second year to absorb the financial commitments that will be required.

- **Summer-dependent employment** could be negatively impacted by balanced calendars. In fact, many teenagers would not be able to work during the day if they were part of extended-year schools that require additional school days or balanced calendars that require class during the summer months. But if intersessions are used this would not be of much concern because high school students will still be able to work during the summer and younger students would still be able to enjoy many of the seasonal recreational activities.

- **Regular maintenance** of facilities, usually dedicated to the summer months, may have to be rescheduled for other times when school is on break depending on the year-round model that is used. Crews would have to change their way of maintaining the school buildings with periodic repairs and such spread out through the year instead of waiting until the end of the school year. In schools with extended days this has been reported as a major concern that requires building administrators to be creative with how they schedule their classes, trying to block off areas in a rotation so that facilities issues can be completed.

- **Existing programs** like summer camp, band camp, sleep away camp, AP programs, and religious camps would be impacted by extended year-and balanced calendars. Because their schools will be in session they will not be able to attend these programs. Administrators can be creative by incorporating these programs into their schools and eliminating the problem. For example, if a student needs to take an advanced class like AP or Talented & Gifted, they could be offered at the school so the student will not miss any time. Other things such as band camp would be considered a school trip and excused absences.

- **Child-care options** may be also limited during the unique breaks that would be used in balanced calendars. But as more and more pre-k facilities have opened up in the last decade or so, the hours of operation are usually very flexible. In some independent facilities, the pre-k schools operate on the district calendar of the town in which they are located while others will be open nearly every day of the year with the exception of weekends and holidays.

In some cases failed attempts in year-round schools over the last few years provide opponents with enough ammunition to confirm their suspicions to continue their opposition against it.

For example, the recent economic crisis has forced several schools to end their year-round calendar programs to reduce spending due to restrictive budgets. One school superintendent in Illinois was quoted as saying, "We want to put our resources, which are getting tighter and tighter, where they will make the most difference" (Dankert 2014).

The recent economic downturn has had a tremendous impact on school reform in which many initiatives, including year-round schooling, have had to be reduced or, even worse, withdrawn altogether. Unfortunately, the nation, in addition to many other countries around the globe, has seen a very slow move to recovery. It is difficult in these tough times to convince the public that such a move is necessary to the development of our educational system, but our students are an investment in the future and providing opportunities to prepare them for that cannot be calculated in financial terms.

Other opponents look to professionals in the field to support their beliefs.

CONTRADICTORY RESEARCH

Some researchers are skeptical that more time will increase student performance at all (Cuban 2008). They point to other studies by educational researchers that have found little if any substantial gains in student achievement from year-round education. My own study even found that year-round high school students actually performed more poorly than their traditional peers on standardized test in California, Illinois, and Texas (Pedersen 2011). But when looking more closely at the data a good many of those schools adopted year-round schooling to address overcrowding issues within their districts, which is why this reason is perhaps the least effective in increasing student achievement and is more of a temporary solution to student population issues.

Other schools have had some negative experiences with year-round calendars that extend beyond overcrowding. The San Diego Unified School District, for example, conducted its own study in 1991, where balanced calendar schools were implemented in 1972, and found no significant difference in student achievement (Wildman et al. 1999). Baltimore, Maryland, had stopped the nontraditional calendar that it's had at Coleman Elementary for the last ten years due to inability to sufficiently train teachers (Neufield 2005).

In these examples, the districts most likely did not perform periodic assessments to determine if the model adopted is sufficiently addressing the needs of the students as well as the district. Effective reform of any kind needs to be monitored and adjusted to ensure success.

In other areas also referred to by critics, student and teacher issues forced some schools to reconsider year-round schooling. The Alabama school district, for example, reported problems with maintaining the athletic program in their year-round school because of scheduling conflicts with other schools with traditional calendars. Consequently, the school returned to a traditional school calendar and resumed their athletic calendar (Zuckerbrod 2007). In another district, Omaha schools resisted the initiatives to move toward a year-round calendar, making the implementation process difficult and cumbersome (Saunders 2006).

In both of these cases, planning and the involvement of stakeholders in the process could possibly have prevented these setbacks from occurring. It cannot be emphasized enough how crucial it is to involve as many people as possible before a calendar is adopted and implemented. In the example of the athletic schedule in Alabama, coaches, parents, and even students could have foreseen problems that would occur with an extended calendar and another model could have been adopted instead. In the Nebraska example, a lesson could be learned about the importance of teacher involvement and preparation.

In almost any type of model of year-round instruction, teacher training will be necessary. The workshops could include differentiated instruction, project-based learning, or other strategies that will engage students in learning activities that have students applying what they have learned. The best way to do this is to have teachers teach their colleagues using a best practices approach.

Last, another criticism that often is given to supporters of year-round educations comes from the belief that American schools, described as falling behind their international counterparts, are trying to mimic what other countries are doing. This, of course, can be seen in the school calendars. Many feel though, however, that foreign schools "tend to stifle creativity, which they view as a critical component of America's economic success" (Bussard 2014).

Indeed, the issue of global comparisons has not been without its own criticism. The United States is unique in that its size and diversity offer no exact comparisons. Therefore, scores from countries like Finland, China, and South Korea are often used.

THE ARGUMENTS

The arguments for the opposition should always be taken into consideration during the planning stages. What follows below is a brief overview of some of the arguments the opposition use to support their stance:

Researchers

- Naylor argued in his study that changing the school calendar had no effect on student achievement and disagreed with studies that praised positive benefits of year-round schooling, stating that the results were skewed (1995). In this research, the author questioned the value of using standardized tests as measurements of success and further stated that in his research the scores of year-round schools did not score significantly higher than their traditional peers. As stated previously, it would be interesting to assess from these studies if the year-round schools adopted this reform to address overpopulation or increase student achievement. Based on considerable studies it appears that the two goals are difficult to accomplish simultaneously and require careful consideration of the exact purpose and intent of implanting a year-round calendar.

- Cooper reported an uneven impact of summer vacation on student achievement in his 1996 research. In his meta-analysis the uneven results referred to the groups of students from the studies he researched. For example, most research corroborates that summer fade affects at-risk and low-achieving students the most. Results regarding high-achieving students were not included in this meta-analysis.

- The literature did not provide a consensus about the relative amounts of time devoted to instructional and noninstructional time in schools in Karweit's 1985 research. The issue of time has always been of great importance regarding educational reform. As has been previously stated, more time will not ensure greater student achievement. When and where additional time should be added should be based on the needs of the individual school and its district. For example, some schools have found success with adding

Saturdays to their academic calendar. In other cases more time can be added during the summer months. Regardless of where the time is allocated, what is of the greatest importance is that the time is used effectively. Traditional lectures, skill and drill exercises, and other teacher-centered activities will undoubtedly be unsuccessful, leading to student and teacher burnout and frustration.

- Matsui wrote that there was inconclusive evidence to support the claim that summer loss affects student achievement and recommends the need for further studies (1992). Additional studies have shown that certain groups benefit much more than others when looking at summer fade; this usually is influenced by socioeconomics. In poorer communities, students, especially at-risk ones, are more likely to experience summer slide than their wealthier peers. In those communities summer slide has less of an effect due to the opportunities students from more well-to-do communities are exposed to such as summer camps, enrichment classes, and other such programs.

- Shields criticized past studies for flawed research methods and analytical procedures and found biases within each study one way or another (1996). Unfortunately, the issue of year-round schooling has had a polarizing effect on people placing them on one side or the other. In doing so they tend to look through the lens of their bias and see everything to support their own arguments. The ideas presented in this book, however, hope to go beyond those biases and provide models that could easily appeal to both sides. In addition, a few models that will be detailed in later chapters also can be viewed as a compromise that would hopefully find support with both sides.

- Burgoyne found conflicting evidence that refuted the notion that teachers experienced less burnout in year-round schools (1997). As stated previously, teacher, as well as student, burnout is a serious consideration that should be addressed. If teachers are forced to add more time doing the same traditional teaching burnout will most definitely occur. This is why professional development integrating technology, project-based learning, and student-centered activities will decrease, and hopefully, eliminate the possibility of teacher and student frustration.

- A cost-effectiveness analysis study was conducted by Dossett and Munoz between academic achievement and costs in both single-track year-round and traditional calendar schools and concluded that year-round calendar schools had higher expenditures per pupil than did schools with traditional calendars (2000). In almost all models of year-round schooling there will be additional costs that must be taken into consideration. These costs range from minimal, in the case of Summer-Based Learning Labs to expensive, which would be an extended calendar that adds more days for students as well as teachers.

- Lamy found that student achievement has more to do with home factors than anything else (2003). The details of this study lead back to the discussion of Matsui's findings. In addition to socioeconomic status, parenting, regardless of financial status, plays a tremendous role in the student achievement—especially in preventing summer fade. Therefore, parents from a poorer urban area might take advantage of free or low-cost summer programs offered in their communities. It is important to note that in comparison of lower and higher socioeconomic at-risk students, the chances of academic success lean more toward the latter than the former. For example, if a student from a wealthy family does not engage in any type of academic classes during the summer and eventually performs lower than his peers, his family has the financial resources to attend to this matter during the school year with tutors or other support. Unfortunately, this is most often not the case with students from poorer families. But families whose parents take an active role in the education of their children will almost always see achievement for these students.

- Some researchers are skeptical that more time will increase student performance at all (Cuban 2008). Critics are correct that unless quality time is added, little improvement in student achievement will be seen at any level. In moving toward a year-round calendar, training for teachers is necessary to ensure success. Similarly, schools that moved from traditional schedules to block scheduling have seen little achievement unless proper training went into teacher preparation to teach differently than they had done before.

Educators
- Trent found that many educators did not endorse year-round schooling (2007). This can occur for several reasons but usually the biggest reason for lack of support is that the decision to move to a year-round calendar is a top-down decision that doesn't allow for stakeholder input. At the core of any type of reform is a well-articulated vision that is shared by all of the stakeholders. Informing educators is the role of the local leadership and

one that all too often is overlooked in order to streamline the process. This almost always guarantees problems and undue friction. If the educational leaders see the value in year-round education they must do the work that is necessary to have the rest of the stakeholders see the importance as well.

- Scheduling school athletics also becomes troublesome for year-round schools with sports tournaments whose conference teams' school schedules are not aligned. However, these obstacles diminish or disappear from the perspective of parents and students operating within the year-round concept. Using certain models does require the input from the athletic director or his or her equivalent to ensure that proper time is allocated for practices and games. This becomes even more important when the school does not share the same calendar as the other schools within their division.

- The Alabama school district reported problems with maintaining their athletic program in their year-round school. Ultimately, the school returned to a traditional school calendar (Zuckerbrod 2007). Once again, lack of adequate planning will undoubtedly prevent the success of a year-round school. When moving toward the future, some of the traditional ways of doings things will become obsolete and necessitate new ways of scheduling athletic events.

- Baltimore, Maryland, stopped using the nontraditional calendar that it had used at Coleman Elementary for the last ten years due to inability of adequate time to train teachers (Neufield 2005). Training is a vital component to the success of year-round schooling, but finding time to train teachers is always a challenge—even within the traditional calendar. Extended calendar with additional instructional days does make teacher training difficult but creative scheduling could address that. For example, including days into the teacher contract that include training would address this issue.

- One study showed that increased class size lowered any positive impact of the extended calendar (Prendergast 2007). It doesn't make much sense to move to a year-round calendar to increase student achievement and increase class size. There has been considerable research on class size (Achilles 1999). But nowhere in any research has there been evidence to suggest that longer school years would allow for larger class sizes. Many traditional calendar schools moved to year-round to reduce class size due to overcrowding issues.

- Some schools have had some negative experiences with year-round schools. The San Diego Unified School District conducted its own study in 1991, where balanced calendar schools were implemented in 1972, and found no significant difference (Wildman 1999). This study is very disconcerting because the district had year-round calendars for a considerable amount of time. Although this study did not go into detail, what measurement was used to gauge success? The most prevalent measurement is standardized tests, but that should not be the only way to assess the success of this reform. For example, college acceptance, parent and student surveys, SAT or ACT scores, and postsecondary success are all important information that should also be taken into consideration.

Parents

- Parents from one Ohio district opposed the year-round calendar and stated that it unfairly disrupted their schedules (O'Donnell 2014). Allowing parents and other community members to play a role in the development of a year-round calendar will greatly improve the chances of it being more widely accepted by the public. As educational leaders would most likely agree, it is impossible to think of everything when trying to implement a new initiative. Involving others in the process greatly increases the chances that all problems could be addressed at the planning stages instead of when it is already under way and difficult to modify.
- Graduation requirements forced a Florida school district to year-round schooling, which angered many parents (Bolden 2014). Schools across the country have been facing increasing graduation requirements over the last few years. Classes such as informational technology, financial literacy, twenty-first century skills, and career planning to name just a few, have been enforced in the hopes of better preparing students for their futures. Unfortunately, this causes other classes, like electives in the arts and humanities, to be limited. Although it was not satisfactorily dealt with in this district, year-round schools could become creative with their schedules to accommodate the increasing demands of the state boards of education. Most mandates have minute or hour minimum requirements for classes. Required classes could be offered during the summers, much like a summer intersession college class, so that student schedules are freed up during the other ten months of instruction.

- A Nevada district that changed to year-round schooling to address over-crowding found parents protesting the decision (Duran 2007). Parents will most likely protest reasons for overcrowding because this situation forces the discussion of whether additional schools need to be built. Overcrowding, though, is rarely something that happens overnight. Most district leaders monitor student populations on a regular basis to anticipate trends and ensure that the appropriate resources are available. By the time a school has become overcrowded, several years' worth of strategies should have been in place.
- A North Carolina district's parents formally demonstrated to show their opposition to changing their elementary schools to year-round for overcrowding reasons (ABC 2013). In much the same case as the previous example, the more the parents are aware of the state of the district, the less shocked they will be when certain measures will need to be taken to solve problems. Under most circumstances, however, parents will usually become agitated when they find out that their children's schedule will be changed to accommodate an increasing student population. This could mean split schedule and academic calendars that may not be consistent with other schools in the same district.

Business Community
- Concern against year-round schooling often stems from traditional calendar advocacy groups with issues such as children attending summer camps, extended travel for family vacations, and summer employment for students (Cook 2005). Although there is some truth to this concern, especially when looking at calendars that extend the school year, there is still plenty of time for summer break. There is also not just one type of year-round calendar that a school or district must choose. There are several models of which at least one could accommodate even the greatest of skeptics. Parents become disgruntled when year-round school are implemented by top-down decisions with very little time to prepare to adjust to the new schedules. Long-range planning or possibly phasing in calendar reform could ease the adjustment and allow families to plan accordingly.
- The International Association of Amusement Parks and Attractions (IAAPA) is the largest international trade association for permanently situ-

ated amusement facilities worldwide and is dedicated to the preservation and prosperity of the amusement industry. They have consistently lobbied state legislators so that schools do not start before Labor Day and end by Memorial Day so that students sixteen or older can be employed in these industries. Virginia and North Carolina are examples of where IAAPA has been successful (IAAPA 2008). Many of the summer-related businesses fear year-round education because of the negative effect it could have on their workforce and revenues. Adolescent work experience is very important in many schools, specifically at the secondary levels. Schools are advised to take this into consideration. Compromises could be made with high school students participating in cooperative education courses by earning credits for their work experiences. With an assigned teacher periodically monitoring the students' job performance, business owners could have surprisingly better workers than they encountered without the schools involved. It is only through using creativity and problem solving skills can some of the obstacles that occur be overcome.

Students
▪ Some opponents are students themselves who simply base their opposition on the fear of what will happen. For example, one online article simply titled, "Year-round school ought to be banned" was written by a sixth grade middle school student who felt that "Year-round schooling should be banned because it is disruptive to summer." The student finishes her plea by stating that "Year-round schooling is like prison—kids are restricted to classrooms summer day after summer day" (Guizar 2014). Many educational reform initiatives leave students out of the planning and implementation process. This is very unfortunate because they can provide important insight into issues that may not be readily apparent to educational leaders. Even younger children can provide powerful feedback that can be used to strengthen any initiative. The more they are involved the better the chances that less resistance will be given. This is often difficult to do because in many schools students aren't given the opportunity to be involved in school or district decisions so when they are finally given the opportunity they can sometimes be unbridled. It is always best practice to involve students in as many school-based decisions as possible.

PROPONENTS OF YEAR-ROUND EDUCATION

Studies on year-round education have shown many positive results for students, teachers, and parents. Contrary to what their critics may claim, year-round schools have shown to have positive benefits for cost-effectiveness, facility utilization, and student achievement. Supporters also claim that it reduces student and teacher absenteeism, burnout, student discipline problems, and vandalism (Loyd 1991).

Proponents also cite the research that has been done on younger at-risk students for intervention to ameliorate some achievement gaps (Edmonds et al. 2008). Much work has been done at the pre-kindergarten level to provide interventions for struggling students. Project Head Start, a federal initiative that started in 1964 to meet the needs of disadvantaged preschool children, was created to address the achievement gap. Some schools have extended their pre-school programs to the entire year to ensure that academic gains achieved during the traditional school calendar are not lost during the summer.

From a different perspective, researchers such as Alexander and Wildman et al. believe that schools need to take the examples of other institutions that have year-round services (2001; 1999). Wildman opines that schools should operate similarly to hospitals in that they must remain open all year long. The argument must be reiterated that one of the goals of education is to prepare students for the professional world; having a school year that does not resemble a working calendar seems counterproductive. Although the agrarian calendar did influence many different things in the United States, the nation · is ready to move ahead to a calendar that more closely resembles the world students will soon occupy.

Feedback from the teachers is also important in gauging the success of year-round reform. For example, surveys from faculty members at one year-round school support calendar reform and report having more options and less teacher burnout than when using a traditional academic calendar (Gismondi 2005). Teachers who are in successful year-round schools explain that in a year-round school less time is needed to regain the focus of students than they used to have when they operated in a ten-month academic calendar. Depending on the model used, teachers could also have the same number of vacation days, but spread out more evenly, which helps reduce burnout.

THE PROGRESSION OF YEAR-ROUND SCHOOLS IN AMERICA

This is most likely the reason that there appears to be a national trend toward year-round education—even if for many districts it is only at the planning stages. The discussion of year-round schooling is increasing at the state and national levels, steadily gaining supporters. As the economic situation improves, both domestically and globally, the timing will be perfect for nationwide reform for states to reexamine how they spend their instructional time.

The number of schools with shorter summer breaks has doubled, with forty-six states having schools with balanced calendars (Zuckerbrod 2007). With each passing year more schools and districts are experimenting with balanced calendars or supplemental summer programs to address the learning gap that occurs during summer vacation. Many reformers only have to ask the question of what is happening to students (especially at-risk) during the summer months to know that major change is at the precipice (Ballinger and Kneese 2006).

Finally, there is also a movement of digital-age educators who question the validity and necessity of the traditional calendar itself (Cuban 2008). With the development and availability of online learning opportunities, students are given a multitude of learning options that do not require the traditional calendar or the required seat time that most schools still use to earn credits. Time requirements, based on the antiquated Carnegie units, are starting to come under question when mastery of a subject is much more important than the amount of time a student spends in class. In the very near future the antiquated way of counting *seat time* as a minimum requirement for attainment of credit, and graduation requirements will become a thing of the past. Demonstrating competency in a subject will be much more important because students learn at different rates and speeds.

After all, why should a student who can move faster and demonstrate mastery be held back just because he or she has not provided the necessary amount of seat time in a class? As most educators would agree, this is not how the real world operates, and it prevents students from making the most out of their school experience.

THE GOALS OF YEAR-ROUND EDUCATION

Year-round education is only one of many types of educational reforms that seek to improve student achievement. Most experts would agree that education is in a constant state of reform. It has only been in the last decade or so that it seems the pace has quickened much more than in previous generations. Undoubtedly, technology and the information age have contributed to the pace, as well as the growth that is expected of our students. In this rapidly changing time trying to plan for the future has become a very difficult task. This is one of the many reasons that calendar reform is one of the initiatives that could be used to improve schools across the country.

The overall goals of year-round education cover many areas but can be collectively viewed as

- Reducing summer learning loss;
- Possible remediation for at-risk students who have fallen behind or need additional assistance to decrease and possibly eliminate the achievement gap;
- Assisting students with disabilities (already many special needs students receive year-round educational services as per their Individualized Educational Plans) so that interventions can be put in place to decrease, or even eliminate, deficiencies that these students may have;
- Providing children with safe activities that will keep them engaged in communities where safety is an issue;
- Addressing the achievement gap with all students through academic opportunities that will ameliorate the chasms that occur across race, gender, and socioeconomic groups;
- Providing programs that appeal to the arts, Gifted and Talented, and Advanced Placement programs; and
- Creating a calendar that more closely resembles the calendars of other professions.

VARIETY OF PROPONENTS

Although most proponents of year-round education may have one specific area that attracted them to this reform the most, there could be a variety of reasons they support this initiative. These supporters include teachers, administrators, parents, researchers, students, and other community members.

For the sake of clarity the following categories are provided so that readers can have a clearer idea of the perspectives of the supporters.

- There are individuals who feel that an extended school year will increase student achievement;
- There are supporters who believe that summer fade or summer slide is an academic problem that should be addressed in the schools; and
- Last, there are those who have seen graduation requirements increase over the last few decades that have marginalized certain areas like physical education, humanities, and the performing arts and are looking for new and innovative ways to integrate them once again into the school curriculum for the benefit of the students.

FACING THE CHALLENGES

Proponents of year-round schooling are not oblivious to the challenges that exist and acknowledge the work that must be done to move forward. They are not oblivious to these obstacles and collaborate with colleagues to sufficiently address these issues. Their perspectives usually fall into one or more of the following areas.

- The **philosophical shift** for supporters is not as troubling as seems to be for the opponents. They see calendar reform as a way of preparing our students for the future and view change as a necessary part of progress, especially when it comes to the nation's education system. Much as we cannot prepare our students today for the obsolete jobs we had in our past, so, too, must educators foster learning that is not just in a traditional ten-month schedule but one that exists throughout the year and even after they graduate. Only by constantly learning can our students stay relevant and be adequately prepared for a world that is constantly changing.
- Proponents of year-round education realize that **more time** does not guarantee student achievement. They understand that in order for students to achieve, meaningful work in the classroom must be fostered by the teacher. The misconception that most opponents have is that school during the summer will look like school during the regular school year. This is not true. Year-round schooling can be implemented in a variety of ways that could include additional classes, project-based learning, intersessions, field trips, job shadowing, and work experiences. Unfortunately, some year-round schools do not follow this belief and what occurs is more time with

little to no increase in student achievement. Proponents also don't view time as a constraint but as a commodity. A common misconception is that summer school is five days a week for the entire summer. Who says it has to be a five-day week? A Tuesday-through-Thursday school week could suffice during the summer and accomplish the same things. Creative scheduling that works with the needs of the school community is paramount to success.

- **Teacher unions** could also potentially be some of the biggest proponents to this reform movement. Perhaps the worst mistake that could ever occur, though, is if schools try to force teachers to work extra days without adequate compensation. If it is decided that school days are to be added to the calendar, then teachers should be paid accordingly. If schools decide to adopt intersessions, cyber summers, or Summer Learning Based Labs, then the funding would not be as substantial. But if the days are merely redistributed, then salaries would not have to be renegotiated.

- **Professional development** is vital for any type of year-round education. Whether it is an extended year or any other type of summer program, the traditional lecture style format will not be successful—in fact, many professionals would add that it is not that successful in ten-month schools either. Teachers will need to approach their lessons in a way that allows for student-driven activities and not the old fashioned teacher-centered approach.

- **Teacher/administrator/staff burnout** is always an issue that needs attention. This is why when adopting a year-round calendar a district must take into account all the variables that will go into a productive learning environment. In some cases additional days are necessary and vacation schedules will have to change from the way they have always been handled. In the case of intersessions and supplemental summer programs, the burnout rate should be minimal if it exists at all. When schools or districts begin the planning stages of implementation, this is a topic that should be presented and discussed. Sometimes planning for such situations can provide enough ideas for ensuring that burnout does not occur.

- Some **parents** can be proponents if they are given the opportunity to be part of the decision-making process and provided the chance to choose the type of calendar model that will be instituted at the school or district. As mentioned previously, for many families summer vacation is the tie that binds them together and anything that seeks to prevent this will be vehemently opposed. But if the needs of the parents can be kept intact and administrators can be creative with their summer scheduling, parents will more than likely support this initiative.

- **Student** support is very similar to those outlined for the parents above. Students of all ages value spending quality time participating in projects that are hands-on and applying their knowledge instead of merely testing it. Once again, the type of calendar reform that is adopted should allow for student input, especially at the middle and high school levels. It must also be added that elementary, middle, and high school calendars need not always be the same but the vacation schedules should allow for families to have common time off for vacations.

- Proponents of year-round schools will view **sports and extra-curricular activities** as a vital part of education. In some cases with extended schooling, students who may be on a vacation will have games and tournaments, but this often occurs anyway because district calendars vary. Careful attention to the scheduling of events is needed and the more people who look at a proposed school calendar the better it will be.

- **Businesses** may never fully support year-round schooling but would be less inclined to oppose it if measures could be taken to ensure their teenage workforce through cooperative learning as well as programs that only impact part of the summer months. If businesses partnered with secondary schools so that students could participate in cooperative education programs that allowed them to work and receive credits at the same time, both entities would benefit.

- Proponents also realize that the **regular maintenance** of facilities, usually dedicated to the summer months, can easily be rescheduled and balanced to accommodate the needs of the school and the students. This does not have to be a barrier to reform but needs school leaders to find creative ways for ensuring that schools are properly maintained. For example, certain tasks, once relegated to vacation times, could be rescheduled for evening or alternate vacation times. One of the hardest things to do is to help people change the way they do things. I can almost hear, "But we only wax the floors during the summer," as a response from a maintenance employee as to why year-round education could not work. Moving away for the good old-fashioned ways of doing things can be very uncomfortable but as recent history has taught us, many of the tried and true ways that previous generations relied on are no longer relevant. Thinking beyond those parameters will allow the schools to venture into brand-new territory that is not confined to the perceptions of the past.

- In some other cases, students could have options with **existing programs** like summer camp, sleep-away camp, Advanced Placement, band camp, enrichment programs, and religious camps that could be used in place of public school summer programs. Requirements regarding standards and curriculum could be shared with these programs so that the overall goal of student achievement is still maintained. Creating partnerships with existing programs could be one way that schools phase into year-round schooling. For example, if a district adopts a policy that all students must be part of some year-round schooling, that could allow independent businesses, who adhere to minimum requirements, the option of using their programs as alternatives to public school programs.

EVIDENCE OF SUPPORT

Support for year-round education is plentiful and strongly suggests that the benefits of a revised calendar far outweigh any of the challenges that could present themselves in its implementation.

Additional evidence of support from various stakeholders can also be found in the following examples.

Researchers

- Studies on year-round education have shown many positive results for students, teachers, and parents. Year-round schools have reported to have positive benefits through cost-effectiveness, facility utilization, and increased student achievement. Supporters also claim that it reduces student and teacher absenteeism, burnout, student discipline problems, and vandalism. When students are engaged in learning, regardless of which calendar model is used, there most definitely will be less frustration on the part of the students, as well as the teacher. The real key to modifying calendars does not lie in the model but what is done during the instructional day to keep students at the center of the activities.
- Studies on year-round education have shown many positive results for students, teachers, and parents. Year-round schools have been found to have positive benefits through cost-effectiveness, facility utilization, and increased student achievement. If enough attention is given to understand-

ing the needs of the school or district, administrators can develop new plans to accomplish the same things they did while operating under a traditional schedule. In some cases this could mean even saving money. For example, schools can rotate their maintenance schedules to work around the academic calendars to maximize efficiency. The benefits can be seen academically as well. The additional days of learning at a cost of $440 a year outweigh the $600 cost of retaining a child (Chaika 1999).

- Prohm and Baenen suggested (1996) that shorter breaks associated with year-round calendars make it more feasible to offer enrichment activities and remedial instruction. The addition of more breaks allows teachers to provide frequent assessments of their students to evaluate their mastery of the subject matter.

- White (1998) states that some children do not have access to enriching, out-of-school learning activities during the vacation breaks and those year-round education enrichment activities could assist in closing the learning gaps. This is most obvious in low socioeconomic communities where students are affected by summer fade more than their wealthier peers. Over the last decade or so, urban areas have increased the number of free or low-cost summer programs to keep children focused during the summer months. Despite this increase, there are still far too many communities that offer little, if any, programs for children.

- Proponents also cite the research that has been done on younger at-risk students for intervention to ameliorate some achievement losses (Edmonds et al. 2008). The identification of learning disabilities at early ages allows teachers to provide students with assistance and support. In some instances, these deficiencies, especially those in the area of language development, can be corrected. But progress would not be as effective if a long summer break happens during the height of the intervention when students need it the most.

- Balanced calendars can maintain student interest in learning and intersessions can provide remediation or acceleration (Ballinger and Kneese 2006). By redistributing the way the time is allocated schools, a balanced calendar provides students more breaks but in shorter duration. In other models, like intersessions or Summer Based Learning Labs, students can use this time to take advanced classes or get the academic assistance needed to bring them back to where the rest of the class is.

Educators

- There are many educators, especially those in low socioeconomic areas, who believe that without the assistance of free and reduced lunch programs, many students would not be able to eat. The Missouri Department of Health and Senior Services looked for organizations throughout the state to help feed thousands of children who would otherwise go without meals during the summer months when school is not in session (2014). Similarly, the New York City mayor had concerns about students not receiving meals during one of the winter storms of 2014. Despite the dangerous conditions, Mayor de Blasio revealed in a news conference that the main reason he kept the city schools open, where surrounding district had been closed, was that he felt many students who receive free or reduced-price breakfasts and lunches would go hungry. When taking into consideration that many public schools across the nation have taken a greater role in student health and safety, year-round schooling would address the concerns of what happens to these students during the summer months.

- Gandara (1992) found that teachers' satisfaction with the year-round education program grew with each year of their participation. Some didn't even want to go back to a nine-month calendar and questioned the effectiveness of the traditional school calendar that they once used (Brekke 1992). Once teachers have experienced year-round schooling they will quickly begin to see the merits of calendar reform.

- Gismondi's research was focused on the responses of superintendents who had year-round schools in their district. The results indicated that 53 percent of superintendents reported improved student attendance rates, 71 percent reported improved student behavior, 79 percent said teachers were less stressed, 90 percent said parents were positive about it, and 92 percent wanted year-round schooling to continue (2003). In this study, these districts obviously put in sufficient time planning and creating before implementing the new calendar. When appropriate time is given to choose the right model and account for the needs of the district, it will be a more rewarding experience for all stakeholders.

- Proponents of the year-round calendar claim that it allows students to perform better on tests because they retain information better without a long summer break (Lawson 2002). Consistent learning is a much more effective approach than having the substantial interruption of two and a half months of summer break.

- Daneshvary and Claueretie reported "similar to the potential cost savings from school district consolidation, the potential cost savings from a move to a year-round schedule stems from size or scale economics." Their study in Nevada showed that year-round education "not only produces efficiencies in the cost of capital expenditures but also in the other areas such as operations" (2001).
- A study of the Wake County Public School System in Raleigh, North Carolina, compared year-round schools with schools with traditional calendars over a three-year period and found that teachers responded positively regarding the climate in the year-round environment compared with those teachers from a traditional academic calendar (Prohm and Baenen 1992). In most schools reducing frustration that comes from reteaching material that was lost or forgotten during summer break greatly improves the learning climate of the building. Teachers can often be found stating that much of September is spent reacclimating their students to the school routines.
- Restructuring of schools by means of revising the calendar is one idea to meet the diverse abilities of students (Stenvall 2001). Reexamining how instructional time is spent during the school year also encourages administrators to find ways of differentiating instruction so that advanced students can be challenged while slower students can be given the necessary attention to improve their skills.
- An Ohio educator spoke at a Rotary Club, stating that the future of education includes robots, athletic cuts, and year-round schooling (Graves 2014). Many people are beginning to understand that preparing our students for the future is a much more difficult task than in previous generations. Whereas progress in the nation has occurred on a somewhat steady course, the advent of the technological age has advanced at such a fast pace that things become obsolete or outdated at a much faster rate. Therefore, educational leaders have pushed for critical thinking and problem solving skills that represent dynamic learning as compared to the static approach used only a few years ago.
- Michigan governor Rick Snyder signed a supplemental school aid bill into law for year-round schools to improve early education programs and advanced coursework for low-income students (Martin 2014). More and more politicians are coming around to the idea that year-round schooling is a necessary part of public education. As the momentum continues to

increase, year-round schooling will be part of political platforms placing a special emphasis on early childhood students in particular.

- Cocurricular activities can take place throughout the year (Ballinger and Kneese 2006). Contrary to the concerns of critics that cocurricular activities will be negatively affected by calendar reform, there is strong evidence that refutes these claims. As has been suggested previously, careful planning is needed from administrators to accommodate as many needs of the school community as possible, which is accomplished through the scheduling process.

Parents

- In one school district, parents supported the calendar change to year-round in hopes of improving scores (Baird 2014). It is important that if the goal of year-round education is to improve student scores, there must be a coordinated effort to accomplish this. For example, for schools deciding to use an extended-year calendar, curriculum must be revised to accommodate the additional days and teacher training in implementing the curriculum must also be in place. For balanced calendars that do not add additional days, quarterly assessments, curriculum revision, and teacher training may also be necessary. Last, intersessions and Summer Based Learning Labs programs could focus on courses directly related to test-taking strategies and other ancillary skills.
- A Florida parent sees year-round schooling to be a new adventure for her child (Doran 2014). Many parents today are open to new ideas that will benefit their children and unlike other educational reforms that involve new ways of doing math or any other controversial issues, reorganizing the academic calendar is a simple enough idea that most people can grasp. In the era when a majority of families see both parents working full-time jobs and their children being provided before and after school care from independent contractors, the idea of additional time is one that is not only welcomed but a long time coming.

Students

- In one news article, students from a Mississippi fourth-grade class explain what it's like being in a year-round school (*Times Herald* 2014). Not surprisingly, the students were very comfortable learning all year round compared to the traditional academic calendar. When school districts plan to move to a year-round model they will most likely find that the students at the younger grades are the most receptive and appreciative for the time they spend in school. It isn't until the students become older that more of the resistance tends to occur.

- In another news article, Jacksonville Elementary students were happy to receive added technology for their year-round program (Adkins 2014). One of the best ways to get parents and students excited about changing the school calendar is to add technology to the discussion. This motivates students and sends a message from the school leadership that the district is doing something different with the time they are adding to the calendar.
- Students from an Illinois school look forward to returning to their year-round school (Nevel 2014). Once students begin to see the value added to their education they will become excited about the new opportunities that year-round schooling can provide.

SUMMARY

There are many challenges that face calendar reform and both sides can be very passionate about their arguments. As the nation moves toward calendar reform it is important to take into consideration some of the criticisms so that answers can be found. Most opponents of year-round education cite financial and cultural issues while proponents consider the opportunities to produce better learning environments that will help American students better prepare to compete in the world. It is important to reiterate that year-round schooling does not have to be a one-size-fits-all approach. The goal of year-round education is to decrease summer fade and increase student achievement. How and what it looks like would depend on the individual schools and districts.

The Need for Year-Round Education

Addressing Summer Fade and Creating New Opportunities

WHY DO WE NEED REFORM?

There is no doubt that education has always faced the challenge of keeping up with the needs of the nation. Time and time again the American school system has sought to improve public education through reform after reform. The history of public education goes back to colonial times in which the goal was to teach citizenship and literacy to a burgeoning nation and also saw us through some of its most turbulent times when integration was placed in the schools.

Whatever the problem is—the schools have been consistently asked to address it.

So change is not necessarily something new for educators; as a matter of fact, it is something that is constant.

Therefore educators are constantly looking for new ways to improve education and address the needs of their changing clientele. The need for calendar modification is at the very heart of all current education reform because it deals with the commodity of time.

THE COMMODITY OF TIME

Time is a concept that is morphing practically in front of our eyes every day. Work hours, retirement ages, when we get married, when we start to have children have all changed in this current generation. Many of the absolutes that we had come to know in our history are already obsolete.

For example, retirement means something very different today than it did twenty-five years ago. So how we spend our time in school is something that must also be reexamined.

Since we have been forced to change our view about time, so too should we look to the school system. In 1994, *Prisoners of Time* detailed how the American school system of utilizing time was not the most effective. Under the traditional calendar there is little time available for sustained learning, teacher collaboration, planning, and peer observations. The report states that the "fixed clock calendar is a fundamental design flaw that must be changed" (Education Commission of the States 1994).

The fact is, schools have always had to make changes to improve the social and educational needs of the country. The only difference is that, in the way that technology has grown exponentially, so too have the demands of the educational system. Unlike previous generations, the duty of modern educational leaders is much greater than ever before. Most educational leaders have always been tasked with preparing their generation of students to prepare for the needs of future generations—it's just that the demands of today's generation have far surpassed their previous counterparts. Educators can no longer pretend that the need for summer vacation is an anachronism that no longer is necessary.

THE FUTURE IS NOW

Some scholars feel that year-round schooling will be the natural evolution in America (Weiss 2003). Some indicators of this potential change can already be seen by the growing number of year-round public and charter schools that have been steadily increasing during the last decade (Gewertz 2008). Many of these schools use their year-round calendars as a selling point to attract parents who are looking to prepare their children for success.

Districts around the country are experimenting in one way or another with modifying the traditional school calendar. For example, such states as Massachusetts, Nebraska, North Carolina, and Virginia have all recently expanded their year-round school initiatives in response to positive feedback from the programs.

Researchers have also looked to places outside of America and have found that a longer school year in Asia and Europe is linked to higher achievement

(Gewertz 2008). Some countries have even begun to incorporate year-round calendars into their colleges (Okanik 1994). A year-round schedule is one strong option that some researchers and policy makers feel schools should consider if they would like to reduce the achievement gap of their students.

Currently there are over 2000 year-round schools in the United States. A majority of those are elementary and middle schools with much of the studies based on student achievement at those two levels. Despite the number of studies at the younger grades, there is a lack of research for year-round schools at the secondary level.

As more and more schools implement balanced school calendars for all students, it is vital that researchers look at the performance results of all grade levels to determine if year-round education is effective as well as if it is necessary to be implemented for all grade levels.

THE NEGATIVE ASPECTS OF SUMMER VACATION

The deficits that occur from summer fade most often severely impact students from low socioeconomic areas the most. Some studies even claim that as much as three months of academic setback can occur per grade level (Cooper 1996). Other research has found that children from various socioeconomic backgrounds may make similar gains during the school year as their other peers but those from low socioeconomic backgrounds create academic deficits during their summer months (Cooper et al. 1996; Edmonds et al. 2008; Zuckerbrod 2007).

But the summer vacation doesn't only negatively affect students from low socioeconomic backgrounds. Studies have shown that our high-achieving students in America have been losing their place in the educational ranking in the world. Some studies have found that even high-achieving students can benefit from schools with year-round calendars. Accelerated programs and advanced classes that could assist students in deepening their knowledge of their subjects would provide more rigor to the curriculum.

MODIFYING THE CALENDAR

Modifying the traditional school calendar is one solution that some districts have adopted to not only address summer fade, but possibly assist students in accelerating to their appropriate grade-level ability (Edmonds et al. 2008). Summer programs have always been around in one form or another, but year-round schools afford students the opportunity to learn in all twelve months and have changed the education process into one seamless continuum.

Year-round schooling is not only academically beneficial but also addresses the issue of child care, which is vastly different from generations before. One only has to look to the following indicators to see that the way we spend our summers is already changing and looking for new opportunities.

- The number of families where both parents work has increased over the last twenty-five years. Parents no longer have the ability, or the luxury, of having one parent stay at home to care for their children. This has seen a growth in the child-care industry with parents spending considerable amounts of money for people to care for their children while they are at work. In most families with younger children, parents work until the early evening and require the services of day care, babysitters, and other professionals to supervise their children until they are able to pick them up. Another indicator of parents needing to return to work for financial reasons is the increase in the number of day care programs that enroll children as young as six months of age.
- Summer camps and summer programs have increased. One need only look through the paper to see the variety of for-profit programs that are available to families today. Few parents have the luxury of two and a half months of a summer vacation. This means that parents are left no choice but to pay for summer programs that could monitor their children while they are at work.
- Towns and cities have been tasked with providing free opportunities for students to engage in learning activities during the summer. Municipalities understand that children who are not engaged are not productive. Therefore, explorer programs, field trips, day programs, and other such activities are provided to help children remain focused during July and August.
- Schools are required to provide summer reading lists and other activities to keep students engaged because they are well aware of the detriments that long breaks can have even on the best of students.

MORE TIME: IS IT THE ANSWER?

The issue of providing additional instructional time to students in American schools is not a recent educational concern. As early as 1983, a national report, *A Nation at Risk* (National Council for Excellence in Education), recommended that educators add more time to the day to address some of the achievement gaps that were increasingly widening in the American public school systems during this era (Cooper et al. 1996, Gewertz 2008). *A Nation at Risk* awakened an interest in examining how instructional time was being spent with our students in the United States.

During this period, educational research began to look at how much time other countries dedicated to instruction in their schools in comparison to American students. The results of most of these studies found that many other countries had already begun experimenting with the length of their school days as well as their academic calendars.

A Nation at Risk, Prisoners of Time (Education Commission of the States 1994), and "Tough Choices or Tough Times" (National Center on Education and the Economy 2007) recommended districts look into ways of modifying their existing traditional school days to address ways of improving student achievement and addressing the disconnect between the traditional school calendar and how students really learn. The Coalition for a College and Career Ready America, formerly the Coalition for Student Achievement, promotes innovative ways for students to prepare for life after high school and college (2009).

Many schools around the country responded to these increasing educational demands by experimenting with the reorganization of time spent in their classrooms (Anderson 1994). With varying degrees of success, as well as a variety of models, a number of these initiatives to increase instructional time were implemented in schools across the United States. For example, the Center for American Progress found that in the years between 1991 and 2007 alone, almost 300 initiatives were created to extend learning time in American schools across the country (Gewertz 2008).

A number of these initiatives involved lengthening the school day, increasing the number of school days, or moving to some form of a year-round school calendar. At the heart of most of these initiatives was the goal to increase student achievement through the addition of instructional time (Neal 2008).

The basis for many of these initiatives, in lengthening the school year or extending the school year, premised on a belief that additional instructional time would allow teachers more opportunities to teach their children (Stoops

2007). As educators looked to their global counterparts and saw year-round schools with impressive results, schools in America experimented with phasing in different calendar models.

TWO POPULAR MODELS

The school that adopted a year-round calendar most often did so in one of two major ways.

Some of these schools and districts created a balanced calendar that would take their existing number of days (which varied from 180 to 185 days on average) that were spread out over the course of the year. In this design, breaks were interspersed throughout the school year. The number of breaks and their duration can vary from one balanced calendar to another. The most common types are

- Forty-five days of instruction followed by fifteen days of break over the entire year;
- Sixty days of instruction followed by twenty days of break over the entire year;
- Ninety days of instruction followed by thirty days of break over the entire year.

In the other widely used model, schools increased their number of days from 180 to sometimes as many as 270. Schools most often used this increased instructional time for subjects that would normally have been covered in 180 days. In other, rarer instances, new courses and subjects would be taught. For example, a least one school used a trimester approach to their calendar that more closely resembled a college model, including a mandatory summer session. In these schools graduation requirements were usually increased as well to include the new courses that students were able to take.

But the most important thing to take into account with any model is that more time will never guarantee more achievement. If things were that easy all schools would have looked for year-round schools a long time ago. Additional time extending the school day has been implemented for a while now and has had uneven success. The amount of time a student receives is only as important as the quality of instruction that is given. Time alone will not ameliorate the achievement gap.

If poor instruction occurs during the initial 180 days even an additional eighty days won't be able to improve student learning. More time does not equal success, but more quality time will most definitely lead to student achievement.

NEW OPPORTUNITIES FOR STUDENTS

Calendar reform will bring about new opportunities because it will allow educators the possibility of reexamining how they spend their instructional time.

Although it will be difficult, the opportunity to rethink how we schedule our school days that hasn't been done in over 100 years can provide schools with a much more modern approach to address modern concerns.

Think about it: if given the opportunity, what would the ideal school schedule look like?

At first it's very hard to imagine because our entire nation seems to move to the clock of our schools. Back to School sales, summer camps, and other holidays are built around the school calendar.

Year-round education provides opportunities for students because it can be implemented in different ways. In some cases this may mean additional instructional time, while in others it can reduce the amount of time students spend away from school not learning.

What we do with this added or restructured time is of great concern. Traditional lecture-style classes will not be successful in increasing student achievement or decreasing summer fade. Classes have to be interesting, engaging, and relevant. A surefire recipe for disaster is to teach students in the old-fashioned way. Some districts are even allowing students the flexibility of using online learning opportunities (Chambers 2014).

Summer sessions can be used in many ways that could provide such things as

- Electives classes in art, music, and the humanities;
- Physical education and other athletic-related activities;
- Online learning;
- Academic intervention for at-risk students; and
- Job shadowing and working opportunities.

SUMMARY

Today public schools are in an ongoing process of reform that includes teacher evaluations, Common Core Standards, and many others. In addition to these issues, calendar reform should also play an important role. The existing traditional school calendar is based on an antiquated system that does not fit the needs and demands of the modern student. More time is not necessarily the answer. Research shows that quality time is needed to prevent summer fade and increase student achievement. As students compete in a global market it is important that opportunities be given to enhance their learning, and summer programs can be a great place for this to happen.

Summer Fade, Summer Slide, and Summer Loss

The Negative Aspects of Summer Vacation

WHAT IS SUMMER FADE?

Both extended school day and year-round education seek to increase time on-task, but year-round schooling differs slightly in that one of its most important goals, other than its alternative use as a means to address overcrowding, is to decrease the academic losses that occur when students are out of school for the two months of their summer vacations.

This phenomenon, referred to by some researchers as *summer fade, summer slide,* or *summer loss,* has been described as the lack of student growth, or in some cases academic regression, that students face upon returning from their summer vacations (Cash 2009; Mraz and Rasinski 2007).

RESEARCH ON SUMMER FADE

Since 1904, studies have shown that summer can cause setbacks in students' math skills (Schulte 2009). The phenomenon of summer loss was reported in New York by William White in 1906 (as cited in Schulte 2009). White tested students on math problems before and after summer vacation and reported that some loss was found. In 1919, Garfinkel found less summer loss for students who engaged in summer activities than for those who had not participated in summer activities.

In 1924, Brueckner and Distad examined June and September reading scores and reported some loss with the low-achieving students. In 1925,

Patterson examined summer loss for fourth through eighth graders in reading
and math, but found no significant statistical results. In 1926, Noonan found
only a small reading loss for fifth and sixth graders in his published study. In
1928, Nelson reported summer loss for third, fourth, fifth, and seventh graders in math and spelling. In the same year, two other studies were completed
regarding summer loss. Bruene (1928) found summer gains in reading and
losses in math, while in 1929, Morgan reported that summer losses in math
computation, problem solving, and reading comprehension were significant.

Research was completed in 1934, when Kolberg studied seventh graders
and found that detrimental effects of summer loss affected low performers the
most (as cited in Cooper et al. 1996). Schrepel and Laslett found similar results in 1936 with eighth and ninth graders. In 1937, Keys and Lawson found
summer losses in mathematics and gains in reading in fourth, fifth, and sixth
graders. Lahey's 1941 study showed losses in math fundamentals but gains in
math problem solving. Cook completed a study in 1942 with first and second
graders and found that the amount of studying impacted summer loss.

In 1962, Parsley and Powell researched the effects of summer vacation on
achievement of second through seventh graders and found that students of
average intelligence showed summer loss in math fundamentals and spelling,
but gains in math reasoning, reading comprehension, vocabulary, and English mechanics (as cited in Cooper et al. 1996). Arnold's 1968 study examined
the reading and vocabulary summer retention scores of disadvantaged Mexi-
can American third graders and discovered that students lost about 4/10 of a
standard deviation in reading comprehension scores between spring and fall.
Beggs and Hieronymus compared spring and fall scores in 1968, and found
losses in math concepts and problem solving, reading comprehension, spelling, and English language with a large sample of fifth and sixth graders.

A researcher in 1973 (as cited in Merino 1983) reported results from his
study that found negative effects of year-round education among elementary
students in language arts and math. By 1976, twenty-eight states had some
form of year-round education in one or more of their schools (Mutchler
1993). In 1978, Barbara Heyns studied the seasonal perspective of summer
loss in the primary grades. Her findings suggested that entire learning gaps
stem from summer learning loss.

Hayes and Grether (1983) found that a seven-month difference in reading
achievement between poor and middle-class students in second grade had

widened to two years and seven months by the end of sixth grade. Skeptics of year-round education were reported to be concerned about costs, teacher and student burnout, and whether increased time would guarantee increased student achievement (Mazzerella 1984). In Utah, one study revealed no increases in standardized test scores after one year in year-round education (Van Mondfrans 1985). During this decade, increased instructional time started to become an important issue for educators; initiatives such as block scheduling were started to promote instructional innovations (Cuban 2008).

The 1990s saw an increase in the number of year-round education programs. The year 1992 saw the number of year-round programs grow to more than 1800 schools in twenty-six states. Alcorn (1992) found that scores of third, fifth, and sixth graders improved using a year-round model. Fardig (1992) compared two single-track year-round schools to traditional schools and found a positive effect on achievement and greater gains than expected after only a year of operation. Winters (1994) found that students on a year-round calendar scored better on achievement tests after a review of nineteen studies regarding the topic. Year-round students outperformed those in a traditional system, while the traditional students scored higher in only three categories. Worthen and Zsiray (1994) summarized thirty-two studies and two reviews by stating that year-round students may have a slight, but not overwhelming, advantage. The most comprehensive study on the research of summer loss was completed by Cooper et al. in 1996.

This meta-analysis reviewed the major studies conducted for the last 100 years regarding the subject. The researchers found that thirty-nine studies that they reviewed suggested achievement declines over the summer months. They also reported that large-scale movements to change the school calendar have not been embraced. One study during this decade found that the possible reasons for year-round education were to increase the amount of material that students learn and to more closely fit the lifestyle of today's American families (Gandara and Fish 1994). Another study during this time had shown that some researchers felt that children should spend more time in school (Elam, Rose, and Gallop 1996). Similarly, the Bakersfield City School District also had not reported any significant difference since the inception of the summer initiative (Wildman et al. 1999).

Dossett and Munoz (2000) compared the Comprehensive Test of Basic Skills scores of ninety-five single-track, year-round students to ninety-five

traditional students with matched socioeconomic status and found no positive significant impact on cognitive variables. Cooper et al. (2000) reviewed
ninety-three studies and found summer school and achievement gaps. Kneese
(2000) found that year-round programs demonstrated some advantages over
the traditional program schools.

His study showed that males appeared to perform better than females in
year-round schools. However, the gains seemed to slow down after several
years. Entwisle et al.'s (2000) work with the Faucet Theory, which was first
developed in 1997, suggested that educational resources are turned on during the school year for all students, and then are turned off during the summer months. Their research found that children from low socioeconomic
backgrounds had greater summer learning loss compared to their peers. In a
separate study, Penta (2001) concluded that gains in year-round schools were
nullified when racial and socioeconomic variables were taken into consideration, and also found that gains were erased over time.

In a study of schools in Fairfax County, Virginia, Metzker (2003) showed
that the year-round schedule was an improvement in teachers' working conditions. Downey, von Hippel, and Broh (2004) concluded that the achievement gap for kindergarten students from low socioeconomic groups grew
faster during the summer. Burkham et al. (2004) found that many of the
studies concerning year-round education have focused predominately on
elementary schools, but none have used nationally representative data. Weiss
and Brown (2005) reported the contrasting results regarding summer loss,
stating that the research had become polarized. The Virginian Pilot study
had shown improved academic results regarding their year-round schools
that started in 2003. Virginia reported twenty-eight year-round schools in
their state with speculation about adding more in the future (Roth 2006).
Teach Baltimore Randomized Trial found that summer programs improved
achievement in their three-year longitudinal study implemented at a summer
academy (Borman and Dowling 2006). Nebraska schools opted for year-
round schools for educational reasons (Saunders 2006). Von Hippel (2007)
studied test scores for kindergarten and first grade students in 784 public and
244 private schools in different parts of the country, and found no significant
difference in scores for students in year-round schools compared with those
from a traditional calendar.

A 2007 study by Bianco-Sheldon found that math tutoring over the summer helped improve student performance. In the same year, Hawaii switched to nontraditional calendar schools (Zuckerbrod 2007). Cuban (2008) criticized the previous research on time in schools, claiming that its findings have been inconsistent. Schulte (2009) also reported his concerns regarding summer programs to increase student achievement. Ironically, in 2008, Edmonds found that literacy skills improved in summer programs. He reported that suburban children's reading skills improved, while those of their impoverished peers declined. In the same study, the researcher found that reading achievement remained steady throughout their time in elementary school, but that the gap widened as children moved on (Edmonds et al. 2008).

In 2008, North Carolina reported that it was interested in moving to year-round education for some of its schools (Hayes 2008). The National Center for Summer Learning at Johns Hopkins University provided $5.2 million in public policy to promote summer programs (Gewertz 2008). A Massachusetts school district recently received grant money to expand learning time, and launched a $5.2 million initiative to promote funding for implementing summer programs for their schools (Gewertz 2008). Wildman et al. (1999) found that administrators from year-round schools have mixed feelings about the initiative. Problems such as not having a definitive beginning and end, scheduling vacation time, burnout, and teacher in-servicing were challenges that they faced.

SUMMARY

Summer Fade has been described as the learning loss that occurs when students are on summer vacation away from school. For some students, especially ones who are at risk, these weeks away from school can have damaging effects. By the time these students enter high school they can already be years behind their peers. For other students, summer vacation is wasted time that could be better spent participating in new opportunities and experiences that will enrich their education and prepare them to compete in the global workforce.

II

Year-Round Schools around the World

Examples of Nontraditional International School Calendars

AROUND THE WORLD

A reoccurring issue that is often brought up in conversations about school reform today concerns the way American schools measure up against their international peers. In some reports the United States is at best mediocre when compared to the rest of the world (Ryan 2013). In other examples, our schools fare much worse—especially in math and science.

This is most obvious when compared to countries like Finland, South Korea, and Japan, which have received many accolades for their progressive school systems. Researchers have begun to look to these schools and have found that a longer school year in Asia and Europe is linked to higher achievement (Gewertz 2008).

As American reformers look to find ways to retain their international ranking, one of the things they are looking at is instructional time. Former secretary of education Arne Duncan even stated that students in other countries attended school 25 to 30 percent longer than American students (CPE 2011). This percentage was attributed to the average number of days most high ranked countries use—which is around 220—compared to the American average, which is 180.

At least four east Asian countries—Singapore, South Korea, Japan, and Hong Kong—have academic years with more than 200 school days, and these are also the highest-scoring countries on international tests of mathematics skills.

SOME GLOBAL COMPARISONS

A large number of schools around the world employ year-round calendars. Some of them have a longer school year while others intersperse their breaks using a balanced calendar (Ballinger and Kneese 2006). In concert with this thinking is examining how other schools around the world spend their summer vacations. Most experts are not necessarily critical of having a summer break, but rather the duration of the break is what is viewed to be detrimental.

Mark Hughes at infoplease.com, an education resource website, compiled a brief list of regions around the world and how they divide their instruction time with breaks; it is good to see how they compare to the United States:

Africa

Kenya: The school year is divided into three terms, each thirteen weeks long, with one-month breaks between. School days are from 8 a.m. to 4 p.m. (Hughes 2014).

Nigeria: The school year runs from January to December and is divided into three semesters with a month off between each semester (Hughes 2014).

Asia

China: The school year in China typically runs from the beginning of September to mid-July. Summer vacation is generally spent in summer classes or studying for entrance exams (Hughes 2014).

Japan: Most Japanese schools run on a trimester schedule with the school year from April to March, with breaks for summer, winter, and spring separating the three terms (Hughes 2014).

South Korea: The school year runs from March to February and is divided into two semesters that are from March to July and September to February (Hughes 2014).

Australia

Students in Australia attend school for 200 days a year that span from January to December. Summer vacation lasts from mid-December to late January. Their school year is divided into four terms, with each term lasting nine to eleven weeks (Hughes 2014).

Europe

England: The British summer break is shorter than America's and is being recommended to go from six to seven weeks to four (Ballinger 2006).

Finland: Finnish schools have ten to eleven weeks of summer vacation (School Holidays Europe 2014).

France: The school year goes from August to June and is divided into four seven-week terms, with one to two weeks of vacation between (Hughes 2014).

Russia: The school year runs from September to May with a three-month summer vacation (Hughes 2014).

Middle East

Iran: Students in Iran go to school for ten months a year, or about 200 active days, from September to June (Hughes 2014).

Israel: As far as the world is concerned, Israel is leading the way in terms of calendar reform. They are in the midst of phasing in mandatory summer programs that parents are required to pay for. Although there has been some opposition, the government is moving ahead with plans to continue phasing in additional grades in the next few years (Ziri 2013).

North America

Canada: Canadian students usually have from the last week of June to the first week of September for summer vacation. Recent plans from politicians in the last few years have urged local schools to look into year-round calendars (*National Post* 2012).

Mexico: The school year in Mexico runs from September to June with the remaining time spent for summer vacation (Hughes 2014)

United States: Although reform is afoot, a majority of schools across the United States still maintain the traditional ten-to-twelve-week summer vacation that begins in middle or late June to the first week of September, usually beginning after Labor Day.

South America

Brazil: The government requires 200 days of instruction with their school calendar starting in February. This first term of the year runs through until the end of June and the second term starts at the beginning of August (Angloinfo 2014).

Costa Rica: The school year in Costa Rica runs from February to December. Students have vacation for about two months, from December to February, and a few weeks off in July (Hughes 2014).

SUMMARY

Many of the higher-performing schools around the world appear to have a minimum of 200 days of instruction in their academic calendars. Most countries try to reduce the amount of time out of school, which usually amount to no more than a month of vacation. As American reformers look to their international peers, the way they allocate their breaks will be relevant and important information. Surprisingly, schools in Finland have a summer break that is similar to the one found in the traditional calendars in the United States. In other countries, like Israel and Canada, however, they are creating new programs to engage students in learning during the summer months.

7

Year-Round Schools in America

Types of Calendar Reform

SCHOOL CALENDARS

Currently in America, most school calendars still average approximately 180 days, with some small breaks during the year and a summer vacation that could last anywhere from ten to twelve weeks. In comparison, several studies have reported that nations with more than 180 instructional days and/or that have calendars that are year-round have outperformed American schools (Farbman and Kaplan 2005). Some public, private, and charter schools in the United States have responded to this educational dilemma by taking steps to extend their school days and/or school year in order to take measures to boost student achievement (Neal 2008).

In 2005, close to 2,300 public schools in the United States followed some form of a balanced schedule (St. Gerard 2007). More recent data suggests that over 3,000 schools in the United States have adopted some form of year-round calendar. Over the course of the last several years, pre-k programs funded by the federal government for special needs students require year-round education.

Many of these schools were "designated" year-round and still operated in the same districts with other schools that followed traditional calendars. Other programs to increase instructional time, such as classes offered after school or on Saturdays, have had varying degrees of success, but many school districts embraced year-round education as a concrete means to increase academic achievement (Aronson 1995).

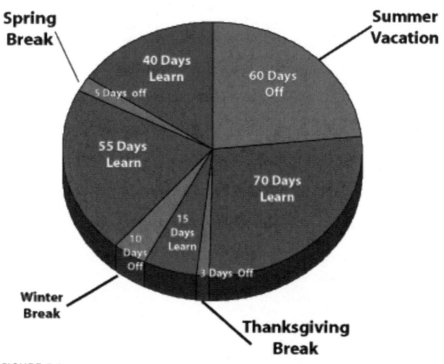

FIGURE 7.1
Traditional calendar.

ALTERNATIVE SCHOOL CALENDARS

Over the last few decades, numerous types of alternative school calendars have been instituted in various parts of the country to reform schools (Ballinger 1998). Although there are many different variations of alternate calendars, year-round schooling is most often implemented in public schools in one of two major models to address the goal of increasing time on task and improving student achievement (Cooper et al. 1996). Countries like the United Kingdom, Germany, France, Russia, Australia, Japan, and South Korea have shorter summer vacations (Ballinger and Kneese 2006).

Balanced calendars can be found in forty-six of the fifty states and at all levels of instruction from elementary to high school (Ballinger and Kneese 2006). Although they may not receive a tremendous amount of press, year-round schools are increasing in number. One site reports the number of year-round schools in the United States at 3,181.

YEAR-ROUND EDUCATION MODELS IN AMERICA

The first model provides additional days to the existing school calendar. For example, a school that originally had 180 school days, which is the American average, would perhaps increase that number to 220 days or more. The exact number of days added to the calendar varies from district to district, as well as from state to state. This approach tends to have more breaks throughout the year, but in shorter amounts of time than the current traditional model (Cooper et al. 1996).

One example of a year-round calendar would consist of a number of school days followed by a break, such as, 45/10, 45/15, 60/15, and 60/20 (Shields and Oberg 2000). Some existing year-round schools actually provide their students with tablets to complete their lessons (Kalmar 2014).

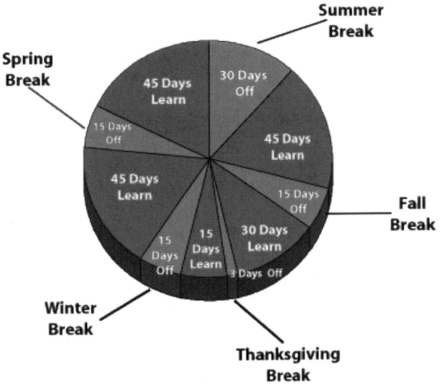

FIGURE 7.2
Balanced calendar.

The second model, sometimes referred to the extended-year model, increases the average number of school days to 220. This model, although not as popular as the balanced calendar, is used to increase instructional days to improve student performance through extending the instructional time students spend in school. Although these calendars can vary from district to district, the diagram below details how a typical one could look.

Last, there are variations of the previous two calendars, often referred to as multitrack calendars, which are used to accommodate overcrowding within the school. In this schedule a portion of the school population is always on break while the remainder is in school. This can enable up to a 20 percent or more increase in student population. In most cases this is used as a temporary solution while the district decides whether new facilities need to be built or if alternative placement will be the most appropriate. Below is an example of what one multitrack calendar could look like:

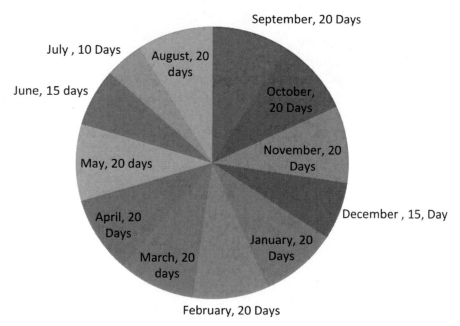

FIGURE 7.3
Extended year calendar.

Table 7.1.

Month	RED TRACK	BLUE TRACK	GREEN TRACK	YELLOW TRACK
September	On break	In session	In session	In session
October	In session	On break	In session	In session
November	In session	In session	On break	In session
December	In session	In session	In session	On break
January	On break	In session	In session	In session
February	In session	On break	In session	In session
March	In session	In session	On break	In session
April	In session	In session	In session	On break
May	On break	In session	In session	In session
June	In session	On break	In session	In session
July	In session	In session	On break	In session
August	In session	In session	In session	On break

SUMMARY

Year-round calendars are being implemented in more than 3,000 schools across the United States at the elementary middle and secondary levels. There is no standard calendar for the nation that is based on state or even local needs. A balanced calendar takes the same number of days from a traditional calendar and spreads them more evenly over the course of the year. In this scenario students will have more breaks, but they will be shorter in duration than the traditional eight-to-ten week summer vacation. The scheduling and number of breaks is based on state and sometimes local decisions. Federal mandates already require that students who receive specialized services be provided year-round education. Although there are other variations of balanced calendars, the two models that represent the majority of year-round schools in the United States are the balanced and the extended-year calendar. A third calendar, called the multitrack, is usually used for schools with an overcrowding student population. The decision as to which model to adopt is most often influenced by the unique instructional, contractual, and economic needs and/or limitations of the district or the particular state.

III

Calendar Reform Models

THE FOUR MODELS OF YEAR-ROUND EDUCATION PROGRAMS

What follows are the two models discussed previously with two additional ones that are less well known. As will be explained, the latter two models are really just variations of the previously covered calendars but have the advantage that they are much more flexible and could easily be phased into any school or district employing a traditional calendar. Each section is detailed to provide the reader with a better understanding of what each model would look like in practice.

EXTENDED-YEAR CALENDAR

This calendar increases the number of school days in an existing school calendar. For example, the average length of the American public school calendar would be increased from180 to 220 days. There are a variety of ways this can be done—by using a trimester approach or simply increasing the number of hours spent in each subject.

Extending the number of days for students can

- Decrease summer fade;
- Increase the amount of instructional time; and
- Create additional learning opportunities during the summer.

Table 8.1. Sample Extended-Year Calendar

Month	Approximate Number of Instructional Days	Sample Activities
September	20	Beginning of school year—opening exercises; first day of classes
October	15	Fall break
November	20	Quarterly assessments; Thanksgiving break
December	15	Winter break
January	20	New Year's break
February	20	Mid-school year; mid-term examinations
March	20	
April	15	Spring break
May	20	Quarterly assessments
June	15	Summer break
July	20	
August	20	Closing of school year—final examinations, graduation; moving-up exercises

Some of the disadvantages associated with implementing this type of calendar in schools are

- Additional expenditures associated with salaries, utilities, and other expenses;
- Difficulty with maintaining the school due to decreased noninstructional time;
- Resistance from certain interest groups; and
- Cultural and historical issues associated with summer vacation that make it difficult for some to conceive of having instruction during the months of July and August.

BALANCED CALENDAR

This approach takes the existing number of days and redistributes them in a twelve-month period. By using this calendar students would start their school year in September and end it in August but have many more breaks interspersed throughout the year.

The advantages to this type of reform are

- Decrease in teacher and administrator burnout;
- Additional breaks throughout the years; and
- Decrease in students affected by summer fade or summer slide.

Table 8.2. Sample Balanced Calendar

Month	Approximate Number of Instructional Days	Sample Activities
August	15	Beginning of school year—opening exercises; first day of classes
September	20	
October	10	Quarterly assessments; Fall Break
November	15	Thanksgiving Break
December	15	Winter break
January	20	Mid-school year; mid-term examinations
February	20	
March	20	
April	10	Quarterly assessments; spring break
May	20	
June	15	Closing of school year—final examinations, graduation; moving-up exercises
July	0	Summer break

Some of the disadvantages associated with this type of calendar include

- Parental resistance to losing summer vacation;
- Limited time for summer repairs; and
- Summer interest groups would not be able to utilize teen workforce.

INTERSESSIONS

This approach most closely resembles the types of supplemental summer programs that are already used by public schools as well as private businesses such as day camps, advanced placement courses, and colleges' summer sessions. This model is the least intrusive and could be used in a variety of different ways.

For example, districts could require students take one or both of the intersessions. Also, intersessions could be phased by starting at the early childhood level and increasing over time. Last, intersession could be potentially "outsourced" to independent businesses to adhere to district requirements.

For example, students taking academic courses may be required to submit curricula to ensure that it adheres to district criteria. Programs that involve physical education may be required to adhere to the respective state's physical education curriculum standards. This may seem cumbersome at first but most businesses, if presented with the choice of turning away business or ensuring profits, will comply with these requests.

Intersessions are recommended to be approximately three hours in length. Schools could have the flexibility to have one intersession or two. The first would be in July, while the other would be in August. Each class is recommended to be a length that equals the time a student would spend in a semester course that meets once a day for half of a traditional school year. Districts seeking to conserve spending may be creative with their scheduling, which could be achieved in very different ways:

Table 8.3. Intercession Options

Intersession Option 1: Single AM Sessions

Session	Month	Hours
Summer Session 1	July	9 a.m.–12 p.m.
Summer Session 2	August	9 a.m.–12 p.m.

Intersession Option 2: Single PM Sessions

Session	Month	Hours
Summer Session 1	July	1 p.m.–3 p.m.
Summer Session 2	August	1 p.m.–3 p.m.

Intersession Option 3: Two Intersession Double Sessions

Session	Month	Hours
AM Summer Session 1	July	9 a.m.–12 p.m.
PM Summer Session 1	July	1 p.m.–3 p.m.
AM Summer Session 2	August	9 a.m.–12 p.m.
PM Summer Session 2	August	1 p.m.–3 p.m.

Intersession Option 4: One July Intersession Double Session

Session	Month	Hours
AM Summer Session 1	July	9 a.m.–12 p.m.
PM Summer Session 1	July	1 p.m.–3 p.m.

Intersession Option 5: One August Intersession Double Session

Session	Month	Hours
AM Summer Session 1	August	9 a.m.–12 p.m.
PM Summer Session 1	August	1 p.m.–3 p.m.

The advantages to intersessions include

- More flexibility with vacation schedules;
- A variety of programs at different levels for at-risk and high-achieving students;
- Job experience and volunteerism; and
- Students being required to take one or both courses depending on the district's choice.

The disadvantages to this type of calendar include

- Expenses for curriculum development and teacher salaries;
- Initial difficulty partnering with other groups and agencies; and
- The need for new and exciting curricula that keep students interested and engaged.

Table 8.4. Sample Intersession Calendar

Month	Approximate Number of Instructional Days	Examples of Activities
September	20	Beginning of school year—opening exercises; first day of classes
October	20	
November	20	Quarterly assessments; Thanksgiving break
December	15	Winter break
January	20	Mid-school year; mid-term examinations
February	20	
March	20	
April	15	Quarterly assessments; spring break
May	20	
June	15	Closing of school year—final examinations, graduation; moving-up exercises
July	20	Summer Intersession I—Robotics; drama; advanced placement prep; physical education; art; television production; media; music; job shadowing; cooperative education; ROTC; teacher assistant program; work study programs; enrichment; remediation; or make-up courses.
August	20	Summer Intersession II—Robotics; drama; advanced placement prep; physical education; art; television production; media; music; job shadowing; cooperative education; ROTC; teacher assistant program; work study programs; enrichment; remediation; or make-up courses

SUMMER BASED LEARNING LABS

This is the least intrusive of all approaches and would look more like work-shops than traditional classes that have been previously detailed. Whereas the time used in intersessions would be comparable to what could be learned in a traditional semester course, Summer Learning Based Labs could run any-where from three days to two weeks and run two hours or more a day.

The rationale behind Summer Based Learning Labs is a compromise for districts that even find intersessions too restrictive. Because of the amount of flexibility of this model, any schedule could be created to accommodate the needs of any district. Schools may also allow students to register for one or more of the workshops.

Last, because these workshops are shorter, fewer costs will be needed for salaries and curriculum development. This the bare minimum any district should provide.

Although the configurations are many, below are a few ideas that could benefit school leaders interested in this model.

Table 8.5. Summer Based Learning Lab

Summer Based Learning Lab Option 1: Continuous Summer Based Learning

Session	Month	Week	Hours
Session 1	July	Week 1	9 a.m.–3 p.m.
Session 2	July	Week 2	9 a.m.–3 p.m.
Session 3	July	Week 3	9 a.m.–3 p.m.
Session 4	July	Week 4	9 a.m.–3 p.m.
Session 5	August	Week 1	9 a.m.–3 p.m.
Session 6	August	Week 2	9 a.m.–3 p.m.
Session 7	August	Week 3	9 a.m.–3 p.m.
Session 8	August	Week 4	9 a.m.–3 p.m.

Summer Based Learning Lab Option 2: Single Month Summer Based Learning

Session	Month	Week	Hours
Session 1	July or August	Week 1	9 a.m.–3 p.m.
Session 2	July or August	Week 2	9 a.m.–3 p.m.
Session 3	July or August	Week 3	9 a.m.–3 p.m.
Session 4	July of August	Week 4	9 a.m.–3 p.m.

The advantages to Summer Based Learning Labs include

- More flexibility with vacation schedules;
- A variety of programs at different levels;
- Short, condensed workshops that require high levels of students engagement;
- Involving students in the learning process and connecting it to things that they learned the previous year or will be learning in the year to come;
- Allowing for job experience and volunteerism; and
- Scheduling based on interest and availability.

The disadvantages to this type of calendar include

- Expenses.

Table 8.6. Sample Summer Learning Based Labs

Month	Approximate Number of Instructional Days	Examples of Activities
September–June	180	Traditional school calendar
July Week 1	5	Advanced placement/honors boot camp; drama workshop; career exploration; sports studies; study skills; robotics
July Week 2	5	Advanced placement/honors boot camp; art exploration; history through film; debate; web development; dance
July Week 3	5	Advanced placement/honors boot camp; music exploration; world language survey; anatomy; math elective
July Week 4	5	Advanced placement/honors boot camp; graphic design; basic engineering; computer programming; science exploration
August Week 1	5	Advanced placement/honors boot camp; drama workshop; career exploration; sports studies; study skills; robotics
August Week 2	5	Advanced placement/honors boot camp; art exploration; history through film; debate; web development; dance
August Week 3	5	Advanced placement/honors boot camp; music exploration; world language survey; anatomy; math elective
August Week 4	5	Advanced placement/honors boot camp; graphic design; basic engineering; computer programming; science exploration

SUMMARY

Each calendar reform has its advantages and disadvantages. The extended calendar provides additional days compared to a traditional American school calendar. Additional days would address the concerns that some reformers have with competing with other countries that have at least 200 instructional days in their calendar. The balanced calendar has the benefit of redistributing the instructional days over the entire calendar year. Intersessions and Summer Based Learning Labs provide the least intrusive of all interventions and can be used in different ways to allow districts the most flexibility.

9

Early Childhood Students and Year-Round Education

WHAT A YEAR-ROUND CALENDAR COULD LOOK LIKE

The early childhood age group is perhaps the student population that would provide the least amount of resistance to implementing a year-round calendar—even from the most ardent opposition.

Students at this age are very adaptable, enjoy their teachers, and look for any opportunity to extend their learning. In many ways it is important to maintain their motivation in learning. In addition to the added value of learning, this stage is also important for early intervention. Year-round education allows students who have learning problems to have them addressed at a point in their development that provides maximum impact.

In many of these cases, if early intervention is provided for this age group throughout the entire year, students would be more likely to require little if any support services later in their academic lives. This would be a tremendous savings for districts as the students move through the higher grades. Another cost savings would be for the parents. When looking at the economic costs of year-round schooling, most families already spend money for supplemental day care for their children; the figures can be upwards of $20,000 a year. Because of the need for supplemental care, many early childhood students already are involved in some sort of year-round schooling.

EXAMPLE 1—EXTENDED YEAR

An extended calendar would benefit early childhood students by providing uninterrupted learning at an age when they need it most. Additional days would allow children to be exposed to reading and early math education. More breadth and additional time could be added to the curriculum. In addition, more time could also be given to physical education, dance, science classes, and other academic and nonacademic classes.

EXAMPLE 2—BALANCED CALENDAR

Implementing a balanced calendar for students at this level would also allow them to continue their education throughout the whole year. This model would ensure that students do not lose any of the academic gains during the summer months that they accrued during the traditional part of the school year.

EXAMPLE 3—INTERSESSIONS

While schools could provide their own intersessions, they could also consider partnering with camps and other institutions to ensure that students are engaged in some academics during the summer months. If the goal of the district is to ensure that students are engaged during the summer months, then certain programs could be approved. When making these determinations,

Table 9.1.   Sample Early Childhood Extended-Year Calendar

Month	Approximate Number of Instructional Days	Examples of Activities
September	20	Beginning of school year
October	15	
November	20	Quarterly assessments; Thanksgiving break
December	15	Winter break
January	20	
February	20	Mid-school year; mid-year assessments
March	20	
April	15	Spring break
May	20	Quarterly assessments
June	15	
July	20	
August	20	Final assessments for traditional school year; moving-up exercises

Table 9.2. Sample Early Childhood Balanced Year-Round Calendar

Month	Approximate Number of Instructional Days	Examples of Activities
August	15	Beginning of school year
September	20	
October	10	Fall break; quarterly assessments
November	15	Thanksgiving break
December	15	Winter break
January	20	Mid-year assessments
February	20	President's week
March	20	
April	10	Spring break; quarterly assessments
May	20	
June	15	Graduation; moving-up exercises
July	0	Summer break

districts should also think about the types of courses or activities, whether they must be academic or nonacademic, and the minimum numbers of hours required for completion.

This could include

- Immersion camps;
- Summer camps;
- Arts programs;
- Music camps;
- Physical education activities; and
- Computer classes.

Intersessions allow parents to retain one of the summer months for vacations, family trips, and other obligations while their children still remain engaged in school-related activities during the rest of the time.

EXAMPLE 4—SUMMER BASED LEARNING LABS

Summer Based Learning Labs can be fun and nonintrusive alternatives for early childhood school students. These activities can be supplemental to the instruction during the traditional school year and be used for acceleration, remediation, or alternative programs.

Table 9. 3.   Sample Early Childhood Intersession Calendar

Summer Session	Month	Approximate Number of Instructional Days	Examples of Activities
Summer Session 1	July	20	Field trips; physical activities; arts and crafts; reading; theater arts
Summer Session 2	August	20	Field trips; physical activities; arts and crafts; reading; theater arts

Table 9.4.   Sample Early Childhood Summer Based Learning Labs

Month	Approximate Number of Instructional Days	Examples of Activities
September-June	180	Traditional school calendar
July Week 1	3–5	Physical education; Lego robotics; arts and crafts; math and reading skills
July Week 2	3–5	Dance; science exploration; drama workshop; language arts
July Week 3	3–5	Museum trips; computer class; design; American history
July Week 4	3–5	Studying dinosaurs; math fun; exercise class
August Week 1	3–5	Physical education; Lego robotics; arts and crafts; math and reading skills
August Week 2	3–5	Dance; science exploration; drama workshop; language arts
August Week 3	3–5	Museum trips; computer class; design; American history
August Week 4	3–5	Studying dinosaurs; math fun; exercise class

SUMMARY

Implementing a year-round calendar at the early childhood level is beneficial for many reasons. It allows for academic interventions and extends the
learning that has occurred during the other ten months of school. Parents are
usually receptive to year-round schooling at this level and are much more
supportive of these initiatives. Having year-round schooling at this level can
be very beneficial to a student's development. In providing the foundation for
substantial educational reform, this age group proves to be the best investment for any district.

10

Elementary Students and Year-Round Education

WHAT A YEAR-ROUND CALENDAR COULD LOOK LIKE

Year-round calendar reform at the elementary level could provide additional opportunities for students to continue their learning as well as expand their course offerings. Academic interventions implemented at the early childhood level could be continued in these later grades to continue providing academic benefits.

At this age, students are beginning to move toward more difficult subjects and courses that could be further developed with additional time. Intersessions and labs allow students to explore new areas that they may not be able to during the regular school year.

EXAMPLE 1—EXTENDED YEAR

Extended-year programs at the elementary level would provide additional instructional time that could include a variety of different academic and nonacademic programs to support student achievement. The additional days could expand on the traditional academic programs or could be separated into two sections—the time that would run from September to June and the summer program, which could introduce new course material during the months of July and August.

Table 10. 1.   Sample Elementary Extended-Year Calendar

Month	Approximate Number of Instructional Days	Examples of Activities
September	20	Beginning of school year
October	15	
November	20	Quarterly assessments; Thanksgiving break
December	15	Winter break
January	20	
February	20	Mid-school year; mid-year assessments
March	20	
April	15	Spring break
May	20	Quarterly assessments
June	15	
July	20	
August	20	Final assessments for traditional school year; moving up-exercises

EXAMPLE 2—BALANCED CALENDAR

A balanced calendar at the elementary level allows students to spread out their academic subjects over the entire calendar year. This model allows students to have a continuous instructional flow that leads from one grade into the next.

EXAMPLE 3—INTERSESSIONS

Intersessions at the elementary level could build upon some of the activities that were completed during the regular school year or could include courses

Table 10.2.   Sample Elementary Balanced Year-Round Calendar

Month	Approximate Number of Instructional Days	Examples of Activities
August	15	Beginning of school year
September	20	
October	10	Fall break; quarterly assessments
November	15	Thanksgiving break
December	15	Winter break
January	20	Mid-year assessments
February	20	President's week
March	20	
April	10	Spring break; quarterly assessments
May	20	
June	15	Graduation; moving-up exercises
July	0	Summer break

Table 10. 3. Sample Elementary Intersession Calendar

Summer Session	Month	Approximate Number of Instructional Days	Examples of Activities
Summer Session 1	July	20	Art programs; robotics; athletic activities; study skills; remediation; world language workshops; drama workshop; math and reading advancement
Summer Session 2	August	20	Art programs; robotics; athletic activities; study skills; remediation; world language workshops; drama workshop; math and reading advancement

for enrichment, advancement, or transition to middle school. Students could be required to take one or both of the summer intersessions as determined by the district.

EXAMPLE 4—SUMMER BASED LEARNING LABS

Summer Based Learning Labs could allow for short-term academic and nonacademic learning workshops that could enhance learning and provide

Table 10. 4. Sample Elementary Summer Based Learning Labs

Month	Approximate Number of Instructional Days	Examples of Activities
September–June	180	Traditional school calendar
July Week 1	3–5	Physical education electives; humanities projects; remediation courses; advanced courses; volunteering; robotics
July Week 2	3–5	World language workshops; study skills; drama workshop; music exploration
July Week 3	3–5	Museum trips; art exploration; design; the world of biology; sports survey
July Week 4	3–5	Fun math; language arts; science exploration; dance study
August Week 1	3–5	Physical education electives; humanities projects; remediation courses; advanced courses; volunteering; robotics
August Week 2	3–5	World language workshops; study skills; drama workshop; music exploration
August Week 3	3–5	Museum trips; art exploration; design; the world of biology; sports survey Fun math; language arts; science exploration; dance study

a variety of opportunities for students to explore and expand their horizons. Once again, districts could require the minimum and maximum number of labs for students and could make allowances for private programs offered independently.

SUMMARY

At the elementary level, the extended and balanced calendars allow for more time devoted to academic tasks, where the other calendars incorporate more flexibility for workshops, programs, and electives. At this age, students are receptive to programs that are exciting and engaging. As they continue to gain their independence, they begin to develop their own interests, which would allow them to choose some of the activities they want to explore.

11

Middle School Students and Year-Round Education

WHAT A YEAR-ROUND CALENDAR COULD LOOK LIKE

As calendar reform is used at the later grades, more possibilities that include career-oriented and postsecondary planning can be created. These opportunities could also be used to prepare and transition students for high school and college. For advanced students, this could help them take prerequisite classes that would allow them to take higher-level ones. For struggling students, this would allow them adequate interventions. Last, students at this age group could also be permitted to use job experiences as their summer requirements as well, depending on the model that is implemented by the school or district.

EXAMPLE 1—EXTENDED YEAR

An extended-year calendar would allow students additional time in their subject areas. Schools could also modify curricula so that students would receive the prerequisite skills for their high school classes. For example, seventh and eighth grade math classes could include algebra material so that students could begin to take geometry during their ninth grade year. This could be accomplished in the other academic subjects as well. As students from the earlier grades are participating in year-round education, their skills will continue to develop so that by the time they are in middle school they can be taught material that had been previously reserved for the high school years.

Table 11. 1.   Sample Middle School Extended-Year Calendar

Month	Approximate Number of Instructional Days	Examples of Activities
September	20	Beginning of school year
October	15	
November	20	Quarterly assessments; Thanksgiving break
December	15	Winter break
January	20	
February	20	Mid-school years; mid-year assessments
March	20	
April	15	Spring break
May	20	Quarterly assessments
June	15	
July	20	
August	20	Final assessments for traditional school year; moving-up exercises

EXAMPLE 2—BALANCED CALENDAR

A balanced calendar will allow students to spread out their education over the entire calendar year. This model decreases summer fade and includes more breaks over the school year. At the middle school level, student often have difficulty during the transition to high school. With less time away from their studies during the summer, they will remain more focused for their high school careers.

Table 11.2.   Sample Middle School Balanced Year-Round Calendar

Month	Approximate Number of Instructional Days	Examples of Activities
August	15	Beginning of school year
September	20	
October	10	Fall break; quarterly assessments
November	15	Thanksgiving break
December	15	Winter break
January	20	Mid-year assessments
February	20	President's week
March	20	
April	10	Spring break; quarterly assessments
May	20	
June	15	Graduation; moving up exercises
July	0	Summer break

Table 11.3. Sample Middle School Intersession Calendar

Summer Session	Month	Approximate Number of Instructional Days	Examples of Activities
Summer Session 1	July	20	Fine and performing arts; humanities activities; physical education; high school courses for credit or placement; remedial courses; college classes; world languages; volunteerism; career exploration; work study
Summer Session 2	August	20	Fine and performing arts; humanities activities; physical education; high school courses for credit or placement; remedial courses; college classes; world languages; volunteerism; career exploration; work study

EXAMPLE 3—INTERSESSIONS

Intersessions provide the flexibility to accommodate family vacations. This semester-like environment can easily accommodate the needs of students who want to extend their learning and prepare for high school courses, or who need extra instruction to help them transition to the secondary level. At the middle school level, academic and nonacademic courses could be taken to prepare students for high school, college, or their future careers. In some cases, students might be able to take high school courses that would allow them to take higher-level ones. For example, a student who excels in math might take an algebra intersession so that he or she can take geometry during his or her freshman year.

EXAMPLE 4—SUMMER BASED LEARNING LABS

Summer Based Learning Labs provide opportunities for students to partici-pate in workshop settings that can accomplish academic and nonacademic goals for middle school students. Districts could require students to take one or more labs during the summer and could also elect to approve independent programs. Outside programs, such as computer training, art programs, and other activities could be counted as their summer learning requirements as well.

Table 11.4.   Sample Middle School Summer Based Learning Labs

Month	Approximate Number of Instructional Days	Examples of Activities
September-June	180	Traditional school calendar
July Week 1	3–5	Project based learning; physical education electives; job shadowing; humanities projects; remediation; advanced courses
July Week 2	3–5	Project based learning; physical education electives; job shadowing; humanities projects; remediation; advanced courses
July Week 3	3–5	Project based learning; physical education electives; job shadowing; humanities projects; remediation; advanced courses
July Week 4	3–5	Project based learning; physical education electives; job shadowing; humanities projects; remediation; advanced courses
August Week 1	3–5	Project based learning; physical education electives; job shadowing; humanities projects; remediation; advanced courses
August Week 2	3–5	Project based learning; physical education electives; job shadowing; humanities projects; remediation; advanced courses
August Week 3	3–5	Project based learning; physical education electives; job shadowing; humanities projects; remediation; advanced courses

SUMMARY

At the middle school level the most obvious need is for students to properly transition to high school. For some students this may mean that they can complete advanced courses that will assist them in taking higher-level courses at the secondary level. For other students, extra time could help them to properly transition to high school. Last, other students could use this time to pursue other interests in the arts or physical activities they may not have time to participate in during the regular school year.

High School Students and Year-Round Education

WHAT A YEAR-ROUND CALENDAR COULD LOOK LIKE

High schools operate much differently from early childhood, elementary, and middle schools; therefore the needs of the students are quite different.

Opponents to year-round education have many arguments, but perhaps one of the greatest reasons has to do with how the summer economy would be affected by the reduction of high school students being able to work at the various summer positions. Just think about all of the amusement parks, summer camps, and restaurants that survive on teenage workforce.

Besides working, another concern also lies in what other activities high school students already participate in. Some secondary students spend their summers planning for college and taking courses to prepare them for their future careers. Oftentimes, the summer is when they participate in such programs as advanced placement, college classes, and internships.

Many high school students spend a portion, if not all, of their summer engaged in sports programs to prepare them for the upcoming season. It is not uncommon to hear that students are enrolled in classes for pitching, stunting, tumbling, strength training, or cardio-vascular. For a certain segment of students who look for athletic scholarships, this can be an all-consuming task that takes up a good portion of their summertime.

At the high school level extended-year and balanced calendars could pose a problem for graduating seniors who have to start college early. Since some of those calendars have students attending until August, this could pose a problem. One solution, of course, is to exempt graduating seniors from the year-round calendar.

Last, intersessions and labs would better accommodate the needs of these students. In addition, coursework, community service, and job experience could all count toward the time and be done in a nontraditional way.

EXAMPLE 1—EXTENDED YEAR

The main reason districts would want to adopt an extended-year calendar at the high school would be to improve student performance with additional instructional days. At this age group resistance from both parents and students is to be expected, but if a district is looking to make significant gains this is the appropriate model. However, extended calendars used for overcrowding will most likely not reap the benefits of gains because it does not increase instructional time. As previously noted, the year for graduating seniors should be shortened to accommodate college orientations, Educational Opportunity Funds programs, and other such necessities.

EXAMPLE 2—BALANCED CALENDAR

At the high school level, a balanced calendar would use the existing number of days over the entire twelve months. The main benefit of this model would be to prevent summer learning loss. Once again, modifications to the sched-

Table 12.1.   Sample High School Extended-Year Calendar

Month	Approximate Number of Instructional Days	Examples of Activities
September	20	Beginning of school year
October	15	
November	20	Quarterly assessments for underclassmen; Thanksgiving break
December	15	Winter break
January	20	Mid-terms for seniors
February	20	Mid-year assessments for underclassmen
March	20	
April	15	Spring break
May	20	Quarterly assessments for underclassmen
June	15	Graduation for seniors
July	20	
August	20	Final exams for underclassmen

Table 12.2. Sample High School Balanced Year-Round Calendar

Month	Approximate Number of Instructional Days	Examples of Activities
August	15	Beginning of school year
September	20	
October	10	Fall break; quarterly assessments
November	15	Thanksgiving break
December	15	Winter break
January	20	Mid-year assessments
February	20	President's week
March	20	
April	10	Spring break; quarterly assessments
May	20	
June	15	Graduation; moving-up exercises
July	0	Summer break

ule of the graduating seniors may be necessary to accommodate pre-college orientations and requirements that differ from the underclassmen.

EXAMPLE 3—INTERSESSIONS

Intersessions at the high school level can be used in a variety of ways to enhance the instructional program at the secondary level. For this age group, districts should offer high levels of flexibility and creativity to allow for enrollment in college courses, internships, community service, extracurricular activities, and career readiness.

Table 12.3. Sample High School Intersession Calendar

Summer Session	Month	Approximate Number of Instructional Days	Examples of Activities
Summer Session 1	July	20	College courses; shadowing experiences; remediation classes; AP boot camp; art exploration; survey of music; computer programming; engineering; dance; performing arts
Summer Session 2	August	20	College courses; shadowing experiences; remediation classes; AP boot camp; art exploration; survey of music; computer programming; engineering; dance; performing arts

Table 12.4. Sample High School Summer Based Learning Labs

Month	Approximate Number of Instructional Days	Examples of Activities
September-June	180	Traditional school calendar
July Week 1	3–5	Physical education electives; community service; remediation courses; advanced courses; volunteering; robotics; music appreciation
July Week 2	3–5	World language workshops; study skills; drama workshop; art exploration; science exploration
July Week 3	3–5	Museum trips; art exploration; web design; computer programming
July Week 4	3–5	Fun math; language arts; science exploration; dance; advanced math; engineering
August Week 1	3–5	Physical education electives; community service; remediation courses; advanced courses; volunteering; robotics; music appreciation
August Week 2	3–5	World language workshops; study skills; drama workshop; art exploration; science exploration
August Week 3	3–5	Museum trips; art exploration; web design; computer programming

EXAMPLE 4—SUMMER LEARNING BASED LABS

Summer Based Learning Labs afford students an opportunity to participate in workshops that could help them with job shadowing opportunities and postsecondary planning. Districts would determine the minimum number of labs a student must take. For example, a district may decide that a secondary student must take one academic SBLL and one nonacademic lab.

SUMMARY

Year-round calendars at the high school could be the most challenging level but if approached in the right way it could allow schools to be very creative with their offerings.. Districts are recommended to take their time to articulate their goals for what they hope to achieve with secondary students. If the educational leaders hope to improve their current academic performance, then an extended year or balanced calendar would be recommended. If the goal is to broaden students' educational experience by providing new courses and opportunities, then intersessions or labs could be the solution.

IV

Working within the Paradigm

Summer Camps, Summer Programs, and Summer Learning

IMPLEMENTATION

When considering which calendar is best suited for the school or district, it is best to take into consideration the goals and objectives of the initiative.

What does the district hope to ultimately achieve?

This will be an important step in the selection process. As with most initiatives, if adequate planning is done, then the implementation will not need as much attention.

If the goal is to address overcrowding, the only recommendation would be to introduce an extended calendar that would allow for approximately one-quarter of the school being on break at any given time while the remaining three-fourths are engaged in instruction (an example of this schedule is provided below). As already mentioned, this is usually done as a temporary reprieve while district leaders seek to determine if additional facilities need to be constructed or alternative measures need to be found.

If the goal of calendar reform is to increase academic performance and provide new opportunities that they may have never had before, then any of the other calendar initiatives would be suitable.

What follows is an example of some of the steps in implementing the various models that have already been presented.

EXTENDED YEAR

Action Plan

- Decide on a year-round calendar to address overcrowding or academic needs;
- Clearly articulate vision, purpose, and objectives to stakeholders;
- Hold public interest meetings to hear all of the concerns and fears associated with year-round schooling;
- Create a tentative calendar and share with the public;
- Train teachers and provide strategies to work in a year-round schedule;
- Review calendar at the end of the year to assess effectiveness.

Things to Consider

- Contracts: In most cases contracts will have to be changed to allow for additional work days. In other cases, especially depending on the language of the contract, districts will have to wait until one contract ends before year-round schooling can be implemented. Appropriate financial planning is necessary because increased costs could be as much as 20–25 percent.
- Teacher training: In order to extend the number of days, teachers need help developing instructional practices that would provide differentiation and project-based activities.
- Schedule: This is important so that parents can plan for vacations as well as child-care responsibilities. Contingency plans for make-up days due to weather conditions should also be made in case the school year should need to be additionally extended. Facilities and custodial planning would also be important for scheduling purposes.
- Materials: In addition to salaries, instructional materials and other miscellaneous costs must be considered.
- Curriculum: In order to address the additional days, modifying and updating the curriculum will be necessary.

Resources Needed

- Salaries
- Stakeholders to serve on implementation committees

BALANCED CALENDAR

Action Plan

- Decide on a year-round calendar to address overcrowding or academic needs
- Clearly articulate vision, purpose, and objectives to stakeholders
- Create calendar and share with stakeholders
- Review at the end of the year and modify if necessary

Things to Consider

- Schedule: Adopting a schedule with as much input from stakeholders is important for success. This way the best schedule for students can be created.

Resources Needed

- Professional development for teachers
- Committee members for steering committee

INTERSESSIONS

Action Plan

- Make a decision as to whether intersessions are mandatory or voluntary and if both are required or only one is necessary.
- Write, develop, or modify curricula for intersessions.
- Decide how students or their parents will schedule for the intersessions.

Things to Consider

- Scheduling: When trying to schedule students for either, or both, intersessions, it is important to decide how this will be done. For example, will students sign up for the intersessions? Will the classes be based on grade or age range? For example, a robotics class could accommodate eleven- to thirteen-year-olds.
- Programs: Creating exciting programs to attract students and keep them engaged is important.

Resources Needed

- Salaries
- Curricula
- Resources for intersession classes
- Facilities and operational costs

SUMMER BASED LEARNING LABS

Action Plan

- Make a decision whether intersessions are mandatory or voluntary.
- Decide how students or their parents will schedule for the labs.
- Promote labs throughout the traditional school year.

Things to Consider

- Programs: Creating exciting programs to attract students and keep them engaged is important.
- Scheduling: It is important when creating the master schedule that it maximizes student participation.

Resources Needed

- Salaries
- Materials for courses
- Facilities and operational costs

SUMMARY

It is important when implementing any of the aforementioned models that proper planning is done with as much input from as many of the stakeholders as possible. The first step to any calendar reform is to articulate the goal in changing the school calendar. Addressing overcrowding is very different from enhancing academic programs. When determining the objective of the calendar model, it is important to involve stakeholders in the process. When possible it is also advantageous to involve the students to ensure success.

Schools without Calendars . . . and Walls

Online Learning Opportunities

There is a large movement of digital-age educators who have gone as far as to question the necessity of the traditional calendar itself (Cuban 2008). With the development and availability of online courses, students are given a multitude of learning opportunities that do not require the traditional calendar or the required seat time that most schools and states still use. Most schools across the country still look at seat time as a minimum requirement for successful completion of a class. In the past, this was the most efficient means of determining that a student satisfied the requirement, but this does little to help differentiate and work to the individual needs of the student. In the future we may see completion of courses based on competency, which could occur at several times during the school year instead of only in June.

Most states still require a minimum number of days for the school calendar. In addition, students are required to spend a certain amount of time for each course. These requirements were created to ensure that standards were being met across schools at a time when this was the best means of assuring that a student completed the minimum requirements for a course. But in the current age where technology allows for virtual learning, the old way of counting hours seems to be antiquated.

This concept can be frightening for many educators because it means that in one class students could be working at different levels. This contrasts the system that we have right now, where students are placed in grades according to their age and not their level of ability.

The freedom that technology provides is the ability to allow students to work at their own pace and on their own schedule. Virtual learning can work at any level but would be most successful with the older students who do not need as much monitoring. Regardless of the level, it is important that some monitoring occurs with teachers and that students receive timely feedback.

VIRTUAL SUMMERS
Students could partake in a variety of opportunities such as

- College classes;
- World language;
- Computer programming; and
- Virtual classrooms.

SUMMARY
Technology has advanced so quickly that public education has had mixed results with how they have kept pace with it. The amount of information that is readily available for students on the Internet is staggering; teachers are constantly coming up with ways to weave it into their instruction. Some reformers, however, see a future where instead of the curriculum driving the instruction, the students' ability drives the instruction. We are at a time right now where online learning is still in its beginning stages. Numerous colleges and universities like Stanford have provided their course online for free. A good opportunity to phase in online learning would be to provide it as an option during the summer. Even districts that are under economic restrictions could still afford online courses, either third-party or with their own teachers, with minimal costs. For example, think about how the summer reading program could look if students were required to complete an online component at least once a week.

The Role of the Stakeholders

Looking at All Perspectives

In implementing any type of calendar reform it is important that the stakeholders are involved in the planning and execution.

Students

- When age appropriate, students should be involved in the reform process because their needs must be kept in mind.
- Naturally, older students are going to be resistant to additional schooling, but if the additional time is presented in a way that shows they will be engaging in activities, they are more likely to be convinced.
- Even though younger students tend to be much more receptive to year-round schooling, it is still important that they are involved in as much of the planning process as possible.
- Conducting student surveys to gauge their interests could be beneficial to a successful year-round model.
- Involving the students in practical situations, when possible, can be a great way to get support. For example, whenever older students can work with younger peers there is going to be much more productivity.

Parents

- Parents can be one of the greatest obstacles in calendar reform but can also be some of its best supporters if they are included in the planning process.

- When possible, include parents to be part of the schools as teacher assistants, job coaches, committee members, and other roles that would involve them in the school community.

Teachers

- The teachers should be involved in the early stages of the adoption of the calendar model.
- Teachers will be tasked with finding new courses to be added to the curriculum.
- Curricula will need to be written by qualified teachers.

Professional Development

- Teachers will need professional development to help prepare for any of the models.
- Districts will have to decide what professional development workshops can be provided by the local teachers and which ones need to be provided by outside providers.
- In order to stay relevant and keep up with the times, courses may need to be revised on a regular basis.

Administrators

- Vision needs to be clearly defined and monitored by administrators on a consistent basis.
- Administrators will need to find creative scheduling solutions to address the needs of their school community.

Community Members

- Community members need to provide the districts with substantive feedback to school leaders.
- Community members can provide internships and shadowing opportunities for students.

Board Members

- Bond levies might be necessary to increase the sizes of some district budgets (Ballinger and Kneese 2006).

- Board members can find opportunities to explore shared services with municipal buildings.

Businesses

- Local businesses could provide job opportunities and shadow experiences for middle and high school students.
- Businesses could set up career fairs to showcase their products and services.
- Field trips and site visits could be used for middle and high school students.

Colleges

- Colleges could allow students to take or audit their courses for intersession requirements. It would be of great benefit if schools could partner with local colleges and universities to see how best they can utilizes their services.

SUMMARY

The roles of the stakeholders are important to successfully implement any kind of calendar reform. As school leaders maneuver to begin the process, involving others in the planning process can be crucial to the success for a year-round calendar reform. School leaders must understand that the role of the stakeholders is very important and can be critical in the planning of a successful initiative.

Conclusion

The traditional school calendar has governed how families organize their lives for well over a century in this country (Rasmussen 2000). Yet, in spite of this tradition, there is some growing evidence to suggest that year-round schools are increasing in number among the states (Weiss and Brown 2003). The National Association for Year Round Education (NAYRE 2014) reported that approximately 3,000 schools within 400 school systems in 46 states currently utilize some form of year-round education.

A considerable amount of literature suggests that year-round schools are effective at the earlier grades. Research studies conducted by Alcorn (1992), Downey et al. (2004), Edmonds et al. (2008), McMillen (2001), and von Hippel (2007) have all shown that year-round calendars appear to benefit elementary and middle school students academically. Additionally, the meta-analyses of Cooper et al. (1996), Cooper et al. (2000), and Worten and Zsiray (1994) (as cited in Burkham et al. 2004) have all supported these findings with over 100 years of studies that have focused primarily on the presecondary students.

Entwisle et al.'s (2000) Faucet Theory suggests that educational resources are turned on during the school year for all students, and then are turned off during the summer months. Their work strongly encourages that students need to remain academically engaged during the summer months to prevent academic losses from occurring. In addition, Entwisle et al.'s (2000) findings that children from low socioeconomic backgrounds had greater summer learning loss compared to their peers were not supported by this study. NAYRE's primary objective claims that only year-round education can collectively modify the education process into one seamless continuum that more closely resembles the popular calendar of the workplace.

The year-round calendar affords younger students the ability to continue their education uninterrupted and address key learning areas. At the middle school level, year-round education has been used to address the learning needs of the students as they prepare to enter high school. Indeed, most of the research that has been conducted regarding year-round education has targeted these two student populations. But the results of this study do not support that gains are made at the high school level. In fact, some of the unplanned and supplementary analyses show that year-round high school students actually had lower passing rates than their traditional peers on standardized tests.

American public schools face many challenges today as they try to compete in the global arena. In consistent studies, American schools continuously fall far behind many other developed countries, such as China, Japan, and the Netherlands, when it comes to student achievement. Reformers have been scrambling to try new initiatives to address this great educational chasm by developing ways to improve academic achievement. In order to adequately prepare for global competition, many districts have begun to rethink how they spend their summer vacations. Educators have also begun to question the value of having students take a ten-to-twelve-week break during the summer months. With newer climate-controlled school buildings and no need of child labor for farming, the agrarian school calendar has been reexamined, with many professionals questioning the usefulness of the extended summer vacation that was based on the needs of a preindustrial American society. But, as we continue to make progress with year-round schools at the elementary and middle school levels, careful attention should be paid to whether programs should be implemented at the high school level as an effective means of educational reform to improve student achievement.

As state and federal mandates to increase graduation requirements become more rigorous, schools have tried to find new ways to increase the amount of time students spend in school (Scherer 2001). Districts are not only looking to assist low-achieving students but are also trying to increase the performance of their higher-achieving children. In the future, year-round schools will be found in every state and in every district in some fashion.

Interestingly, a 1971 survey of professionals in the field found that 84 percent of the participants predicting that year-round schooling would be in all U.S. schools within fifteen years. Although we are far from that mark, it goes to show that calendar reform has been a long time coming.

The reality of national year-round reform is within our grasp. As schools across the country look for new ways to keep up with the times and remain relevant, they will be forced to look at how they use their time. Year-round education, in any of the models prescribed in this text, could move the agenda forward to providing American students with the necessary instructional time that can once again restore our place in the world as a premier educational model.

Appendix

Questions and Answers

Our district can't afford year-round schooling. How can we still do it?

If funding is a question, redistributing time, as in a balanced calendar, would cost the least amount of money. Extended year, intersessions, and SBLL all have differentiating costs that could limit districts. Balanced calendars require the same amount of "work" time from the teachers. It is important to note that contractual obligations may need to be fulfilled of the existing contract before new negotiations are begun.

How will this affect summer businesses?

It depends on the model that is adopted. Extended year could impact summer attractions and businesses that thrive on summer tourism. The other models would not be as intrusive and should allow businesses to continue relatively unchanged. This is why local decision is extremely important and why a national model is not recommended. For example, in my home state of New Jersey, most shore towns need to have teenagers work at the local attractions; therefore, extended and balanced calendars would not be recommended. Incorporating these job opportunities and requiring students to turn them into a more structured learning experience with a paper or presentation takes this experience to a completely new level.

How do year-round calendars impact students with special needs?

Many students with disabilities in the younger grades may actually already have year-round education required as per their Individualized Education Plans to ensure that they receive ongoing education that prevents any gaps in their learning. Expanding this idea, the older students could only improve their academic performance and prepare them for their postsecondary plans.

Can parents choose to home school their children for intersessions or Summer Based Learning Labs?

This would depend on district policy. For example, could a student attend traditional school but not take science because he is being home-schooled? Districts should be prepared for this question and clearly explain what constitutes a third-party alternative to their requirements and what doesn't.

How will year-round education benefit students academically?

Year-round education reduces summer fade and the amount of time students spend away from school; students can benefit from fewer academic interruptions. Those students participating in intersessions and Summer Based Learning Labs will be able to enroll in nontraditional courses that could prepare them for their futures.

Is there an option for students to study abroad?

It is recommended that districts always provide options for students to explore outside of the curriculum. In each instance, activities could be required, such as research papers or presentations that would support the learning objectives of such an activity.

Do schools already use Summer Based Learning Labs?

Not exactly. This is a term created by this author to include the variety of different instructional activities that districts around the country already have in place.

Does a district have to make intersessions and Summer Base Learning Labs mandatory or can they be just voluntary?

That depends on the financial situation as well as the academic goals of the individual district. Both of these models could be introduced on a voluntary *basis with the intent making them mandatory in future years. This can help in the transition of a community toward a year-round calendar.*

If year-round calendars are implemented in our district, are standardized test scores guaranteed to improve?

That depends on the goal of the district. To increase standardized test scores, extended or balanced calendars should yield the best results. If districts are looking for a more comprehensive educational goal, intersessions and labs are recommended.

If only one month is added during the summer is this really year-round education?

If the goal is to decrease the amount of time students spend away from academic instruction, then yes, it is effective. Although other professionals may disagree, year-round education should not be a one-size-fits-all approach. Because of the unique needs of each individual school, each location should make its own determination regarding what is best for its students.

What if parents don't want to participate?

Buy-in is extremely important but does not always happen. If a district is able to clearly identify its goal in calendar reform and works with stakeholders from the very beginning stages, opposition could be decreased. When parents see the benefits of the new initiative they will be more supportive. Last, pilot programs are always recommended, especially if they are done at first on a voluntary basis.

Most of the students in our district already attend some kind of summer camp or supplemental classes on their own; why should districts then have to implement a year-round program if this is already being accomplished indirectly by the parents?

Districts should provide some guidelines regarding what would be accepted and what would not. The guidelines should be clear and leave ample room for appeals to an appointed committee.

Our district started one model and thinks we have to change it to another. Is this the right thing to do?

Change is not necessarily a bad thing. The worst thing to do, though, would be to fail to communicate this to the students and parents, explaining what went wrong and how it is going to be corrected. Stakeholders hate negative surprises and should always be informed of what could potentially happen with their children.

Can a district use noncertified teachers to teach elective courses?

In most cases the state departments of education make these decisions, but there could be many ways to help accomplish this. For example, a community member who can provide supplemental classes about the legal profession could team teach with a certified teacher from the district to ensure that credits can be attained.

Can we charge the parents tuition for year-round programs?

It depends on the district. As has been mentioned previously, other countries around the world have already begun to charge parents for the additional instructional time provided during the summer months. Requiring parents to pay supplemental fees would depend on the state and local legislation.

Does year-round education have to be mandated by the state?

No. Many districts have adopted year-round calendars independent of the state department of education. Most departments of education, however, will provide recommendations on modified calendars that districts could adopt.

What if students show resistance?

If proper planning is done and students are involved in the input, they will be less likely to resist. If students are also given the chance to choose what learning activity they will be involved in, they will be more apt to accept the calendar reform.

Should a school or district pilot a program first before they implement school-wide or district-wide?

I am always a big fan of piloting programs, though it is not mandatory. It accomplishes two goals. First, it provides insight into possible problems and challenges that could occur in implementing the model. Second, it sends a message to the school community of what will happen with the rest of the student population. This allows school leaders to modify plans based on the success of the pilot program.

What resources are available for districts interested in moving to a year-round calendar?

Districts are encouraged to look to schools in their state or other neighboring states that are successfully implementing year-round calendars. In addition, many resources are available on the Internet. In recent years, many state education department websites provide guidelines for year-round calendars.

Sometimes parents have their own businesses where they need their children to work; how can this be done with a year-round calendar?

This determination should be a local issue that clearly delineates what is accepted and what is not. Job experience could be an excellent opportunity to develop a variety of career skills. If a district decides to permit these experiences, it is recommended that a project or research paper be required as well.

What happens with transfer students?

Transfer students from schools with alternate calendars are always a concern, but should follow whatever policy is already in place in the district. Policies should provide timelines and cutoff dates of what happens when a student transfers into the district.

What if a district loses funding a few years into their year-round program?

Unforeseen economic crises can always occur, but the suspension of the program should only be the last resort. In dire times, districts may look to reducing the number of days or hours to help minimize costs.

Can college courses be used as well?

There are two issues with this question. One involves whether a student can attend the course and receive dual credit (high school as well as college) and the other is whether an audited course would count as high school credit or be eligible for advancement in the next grade. For example, if a student audits a college course in world history, would that enable him or her to advance to the next level in his or her school? These issues must be clearly explained before a year-round calendar is implemented.

Is it necessary for a district to visit other schools before they begin their own calendar change?

Seeing how other people use year-round calendars is always a good idea. The planning committee, with parent and student members, would most likely find this very useful.

Which model is the best for our district?

The first question to ask is what the goal of changing the calendar is. Is it to address overcrowding? Is it to increase academic achievement? After those questions are answered, then a model could be chosen.

Where is the best place to start?

Starting an exploratory committee and compiling data from surveys, as well as school visits and case studies could be very beneficial in starting out.

Can a district employ a year-round calendar utilizing online technology?

Yes, but with some reservations. There are many new computer programs that are very popular and educational but districts should be wary of online learning. For struggling and at-risk students using online programs as the primary instructional source will most likely not be successful. It is best that districts spend some time looking at the many programs and what they offer.

How do we know if it is or isn't working?

Success can be measured through a variety of data such as test scores, discipline referrals, special education referrals, and parent and student surveys.

Where can a district get more information?

Information is available in print and on the web to assist districts in gathering information. Charles Ballinger and Carolyn Kneese have written books on the topic of year-round education that can be very informative.

Are there companies that would be able to come in and walk our district through the steps to convert to a year-round schedule?

Not that I am aware of—yet. But as year-round school continues to grow in popularity I'm certain that they will soon be available.

Bibliography

ABC. 2013. "Elementary School Parents Upset over Calendar Change." Accessed July 1, 2014. http://abclocal.go.com//story?section=news/local&id=9100685.

Achilles, C. 1999. *Let's Put Kids First, Finally: Getting Class Size Reduction Right.* Thousand Oaks, CA: Corwin.

Adkins, M. 2014. "Back to School for Year-Round Students." Accessed July 22, 2014. http://www.jdnews.com/news/local/back-to-school-for-year-round-students-1.348965.

Alcorn, R. 1992. "Test Scores: Can Year-Round School Raise Them?" *Thrust for Educational Leadership* 21 (6): 12.

Alexander, K. L., D. R. Entwisle, and L. S. Olson. 2007. "Lasting Consequences of the Summer Learning Gap." *American Sociological Review* 72(4): 167–180.

Allington, R. L., and A. McGill-Franzen. 2003. "Summer Vacation: An Educational Setback." *Current*: 3.

Anderson, J. 1994. "Alternate Approaches to Organizing the School Day and Year: A National Commission Examines New Structures for Improving Student Learning." *School Adminstrator* 8: 15.

Angloinfo. 2014. Accessed June 1, 2014. http://saopaulo.angloinfo.com/information/family/schooling-education/school-holidays.

Arnold, R. D. 1968. "Retention in Reading of Disadvantaged Mexican-American Children during the Summer Months." Paper presented at the meeting of the International Reading Association, Boston, MA.

Aronson, J. 1995. "Stop the Clock: Ending the Tyranny of Time in Education." Accessed March 2010. San Francisco: Far West Laboratory for Educational Research and Development. http://www.eric.ed.gov/ERICDocs/data/ericdocs2sql/ content_storage_01/0000019b/80/13/da/4a.pdf.

Association of California School Administrators. 1988. "A Primer on Year-Round Education." Sacramento, CA. ERIC Document No. 332271.

Baird, P. 2014. "Parents, Teachers Support Year-Round School at Sunset Park Elementary." Accessed July 2, 2014. http://www.starnewsonline.com/ article/20140314/ARTICLES/140319791.

Ballinger, C. 1998. "Rethinking the School Calendar." *Educational Leadership* 45: 5.

Ballinger, C., and C. Kneese. 2006. *School Calendar Reform: Learning in All Seasons.* Lanham, MD: Rowman & Littlefield Education.

Beggs, D. L., and A. N. Hieronymus. 1968. "Uniformity of Growth in the Basic Skills throughout the School Year and during the Summer." *Journal of Educational Measurement* 5: 91–97.

Bianco-Sheldon, D. L. 2007. "The Effectiveness of Math Tutoring to Prevent Learning Loss over the Summer." Doctoral dissertation, Arcadia University. Accessed August 13, 2009, from Dissertations and Theses database. (AAT 3281246.)

Bolden, L. 2014. Accessed July 15, 2014. http://www.clickorlando.com/news/ parents-students-upset-after-osceola-high-school-schedule-changes/26970218.

Borman, G. D., and N. M. Dowling. 2006. "Longitudinal Achievement Effects of Multiyear Summer School: Evidence from the Teach Baltimore Randomized Field Trial." *Educational Evaluation and Policy Analysis* 28 (2): 25.

Bracey, G. W. 2002a. "Summer Loss: The Phenomenon No One Wants to Deal With." *Phi Delta Kappan* 84 (1): 12.

———. 2002b. "Test Scores, Creativity, and Global Competitiveness." *Phi Delta Kappan* 83 (10): 738.

Brekke, N. R. 1992, May. "Year-Round Schools: An Efficient and Effective Use of Resources. *School Business Affairs.*

Brueckner, L. J., and H. W. Distad. 1924. "The Effect of the Summer Vacation on the Reading Ability of First Grade Children." *Elementary School Journal* 24: 698.

Bruene, E. 1928. "Effect of the Summer Vacation on the Achievement of Pupils in the Fourth, Fifth and Sixth Grades." *Journal of Educational Research* 18: 309.

Burgoyne, B. 1998. "The Never Ending School: An Analysis of Year-Round education in California. Retrieved from https://web.archive.org/web/20010414200948/http://www.capitolresource.org/b_yre.htm

Burkham, D. T., D. D. Ready, V. E. Lee, and L. F. LoGerfo. 2004. "Social-Class Difference in Summer Learning between Kindergarten and First Grade: Model Specification and Estimation." *Sociology of Education* 77: 1.

Bussard, B. 2014. "Keep Education Reform Focused on Quality Instruction Time." *It's About Quality Time.* http://www.summermatters.com/xtended.htm.

California Department of Education Website. Accessed August 1, 2010. www.cde.ca.gov/ta/ac/ap/glossary10b.asp.

Cash, R. E. 2009. "Imagine: Education for the New Millennium." *National Association of School Principals* 37 (6): 2.

Chaika, G. 1999. "Is Year-Round Schooling the Answer?" *Education World.* Retrieved March 2, 2003, from www.educationworld.com/a_issues/issues066.shtml.

Chambers, J. 2014. "Detroit's EAA Offers High School Students Flexible Summer Schedule." *Detroit News.* Accessed June 3, 2014. http://www.detroitnews.com/article/20140224/SCHOOLS/302240067#ixzz38aHmT8fq.

Chappel, B. 2013. "U.S. Students Slide in Global Ranking on Math, Reading, Science." Accessed September 1, 2014. http://www.npr.org/blogs/thetwo-way/2013/12/03/248329823/u-s-high-school-students-slide-in-math-reading-science.

Coalition for Student Achievement. 2009. "Coalition for Student Achievement Calls for Bold Action on Stimulus Education Reforms." *Education Business Weekly* (April): 5. Accessed August 2, 2010. http://iirc.niu.edu/Default.aspx.

Cook, G. 2005. "Calendar Wars." *American School Board Journal* (January): 24–27.

Cook, R. C. 1942. "Vacation Retention of Fundamentals by Primary-Grade Pupils." *The Elementary School Journa,* 43: 214–219.

Cooper, H., K. Charlton, J. C. Valentine, and L. Muhlenbruck. 2000. "Making the Most of Summer School: A Meta-Analytic Review." *Review of Educational Research* 66: 406.

Cooper, H., B. Nye, K. Charlton, J. Lindsey, and S. Greathouse. 1996. "The Effects of Summer Vacation on Achievement Test Scores: A Narrative and Meta-Analytic Review." *Review of Educational Research* 66 (3): 227.

CPE (Center for Public Education). 2011. "Time in School: How Does the U.S. Compare?" Accessed June 1, 2014. http://www.centerforpubliceducation.org/Main-Menu/Organizing-a-school/Time-in-school-How-does-the-US-compare.

Cuban, L. 2008. "The Perennial Reform: Fixing School Time." *Phi Delta Kappan* 90 (4): 240.

Daneshvary, N., and T. M. Clauretie. 2001. "Efficiency and Costs in Education: Year Round versus Traditional Schedules." *Economics of Education Review* 20, 279–287.

Dankert, J. 2014. "Peru Elementary Considers Ending Summer School." *News Tribune.* http://newstrib.com/main.asp?SectionID=2&SubSectionID=27&ArticleID=35379.

Doran, W. 2014. "Happy to Be Back: Excitement, Few Tears, Mark Tramway's First Day." Accessed July 22, 2014. http://www.sanfordherald.com/news/x143262627/Happy-to-be-back.

Dossett, D., and M. Munoz. 2000. "Year-Round Education in a Reform Environment: The Impact on Student Achievement and Cost-Effectiveness Analysis." ERIC Document No. ED 464424.

Downey, D., P. von Hippel, and B. Broh. 2004. "Are Schools the Great Equalizer? Cognitive Inequality during the Summer Months and the School Year." *American Sociological Review* 69 (5): 613–35.

Duran, M. 2007. "Parents Say Year-Round School Fight Not Over." Accessed July 1, 2014. http://www.8newsnow.com/story/6455062/parents-say-year-round-school-fight-not-over.

Edmonds, E., C. O'Donoghue, S. Spano, and R. F. Algozzine. 2008. "Learning When School Is Out." *Journal of Educational Research* 102 (3): 213.

Education Commission of the States. 1994. *Prisoners of Time.* Reprint of the 1994 Report of the National Education Commission on Time and Learning. Accessed August 13, 2013. http://files.eric.ed.gov/fulltext/ED489343.pdf.

Elam, S. M., L. C. Rose, and A. M. Gallop. 1996. "The 28th Annual Phi Delta Kappa/ Gallup Poll of Public Attitudes toward the Public Schools." *Phi Delta Kappan* 78: 41.

Entwisle, D. R., K. L. Alexander, and L. S. Olson. 1997. *Children, Schools, and Inequality.* Boulder, CO: Westview.

———. 2000. "Summer Learning and Home Environment." In *A Nation at Risk,* edited by R. D. Kahlenberg, 9–30. New York: Century.

Farbman, D., and C. Kaplan. 2005. "Time for a Change: The Promise of Extended-Time Schools for Promoting Achievement." Massachusetts 2020. Accessed February 2010. http://www.mass2020.org.

Fardig, D. 1992. "Year-Round Education." Program evaluation report. ERIC Document No. 357047.

Gandara, P. 1992. "Extended Year, Extended Contracts: Increasing Teacher Salary Options." *Urban Education* 27 (3): 229–247.

Gandara, P., and J. Fish. 1994. "Year-Round Schooling as an Avenue to Major Structural Reform." *Educational Evaluation and Policy Analysis* 16: 67.

Garfinkel, M. A. 1919. "The Effect of the Summer Vacation on Ability in the Fundamentals of Arithmetic." *Journal of Educational Psychology* 10: 44.

Gay, L. R., G. E. Mills, and P. Airasian. 2009. *Educational Research: Competencies for Analysis and Applications.* Upper Saddle River, NJ: Merrill/Pearson.

Gewertz, C. 2008. "Consensus on Learning Time Builds: Interest in Expanding Hours for Students to Master Academic, Social, and Workplace Skills Is Mounting." *Education Week* 28 (5): 1.

Gismondi Haser, S., and I. Nasser. 2005. *Year-Round Education: Change and Choice for Schools and Teachers.* Lanham, MD: Scarecrow Press.

Glines, D. 1995. *Year Round Education: History, Philosophy, Future.* San Diego: National Association for Year-Round Education.

———. 1997. *YRE: Understanding the Basics.* National Association for Year-Round Education. ERIC Document No. 406731.

Gold, K. M. 2002. *School's In: The History of Summer Education in American Public Schools.* New York: Peter Lang.

Graves, B. 2014. "Changes in Education Coming." Accessed July 3, 2014. http://www.clevelandbanner.com/view/full_story/24863113/article-Changes-in-education-coming?instance=homefirstleft.

Guizar, K. 2014. "Year-Round School Ought to Be Banned." http://www.
thetimesherald.com/article/20140318/OPINION/303180013/Year-round-school-
ought-banned.

Hayes, D. P., and J. Grether. 1983. "The School Year and Vacations: When Do
Students Learn?" *Cornell Journal of Social Relations* 17: 56–71.

Hayes, K. 2008. "School Officials Consider Year-Round Switch." *Tribune Business
News*, February 19, 2008.

Hazelton, J. 1992. "Cost Effectiveness of Alternative Year Schooling." Final Report.
Austin, TX: Educational Economic Policy Center. ERIC Document No. 354629.

Heyns, Barbara. 1978. *Summer Learning and the Effects of Schooling*. New York:
Academic.

Huebner, T. 2010. "What Research Says About… /Year-Round Schooling." *Educational
Leadership*. Accessed September 1, 2013. http://www.ascd.org/publications/
educational_leadership/apr10/vol67/num07/Year-Round_Schooling.aspx.

Hughes, M. 2014. "School Years around the World." Accessed June 2, 2014. http://
www.infoplease.com/world/statistics/school-years.html#ixzz2yzoEdyne.

IAAPA (International Association of Amusement Parks and Attractions). 2008.
"IAAPA, Florida Tourism Industry Lobbies for Worker-Friendly School Year."
Accessed July 2, 2014. http://coasterbuzz.com/Forums/Topic/iaapa-florida-
tourism-industry-lobbies-for-worker-friendly-school-year.

Illinois State Board of Education. Accessed August 2, 2010. http://iirc.niu.edu/
Default.aspx.

Kalmar, M. 2014. "Farewell, Summer: Classes Resume at Dist. 59 School of Choice
Ridge." *Journal Online*. Accessed July 23, 2014. http://www.journal-topics.com/
news/article_33dcb2dc-140c-11e4-b972-0017a43b2370.html.

Karweit, N. 1985. "Should we Lengthen the School Term?" *Educational Researcher*,
14 (6): 9–15.

Keys, N., and I. V. Lawson. 1937. "Summer versus Winter Gains in School
Achievement." *School and Society* 46 (54): 15–44.

Kneese, C. C. 2000. "Teaching in Year-Round Schools." ERIC Document No.
ED449123.

Kneese, C., and C. Ballinger. 2009. *Balancing the School Calendar: Perspectives from
the Public and Stakeholders*. New York: Rowman & Littlefield Education.

Kramer, G. A. 1927. "Do Children Forget during the Vacation?" *Baltimore Bulletin of Education* 6: 56.

Lahey, M. F. 1941. "Permanence of Retention of First-Year Algebra." *The Journal of Educational Psychology* 32: 401–413.

Lamy, C. E. 2013. How Preschools Fight Poverty. *Educational Leadership* 70(8): 32–36.

Lynch, M. 2014. "Year-Round Schooling: How It Affects Students." Accessed February 10, 2014. http://www.huffingtonpost.com/matthew-lynch-edd/year-round-schooling-how_b_4622211.html.

Martin, A. 2014. "Michigan Supplemental School Aid Bill Becomes Law." Accessed July 5, 2014. http://riponadvance.com/news/michigan-supplemental-school-aid-bill-becomes-law/7306.

Matsui, B. I. 1992. "Comparison of Year-Round vs. Traditional Sequences on Selected Achievement Variables. Doctoral dissertation, University of Southern California, 1992. Dissertation Abstracts International, 53-12, 4156.

Mazzerella, J. A. 1984. "Longer Day, Longer Year: Will They Make a Difference?" *Principal* 63: 14.

McMillen, B. 2001. "A Statewide Evaluation of Academic Achievement in Year-Round Schools." *Journal of Educational Research* 95 (2): 67.

Merino, B. J. 1983. "The Impact of Year-Round Schooling: A Review." *Urban Education* 18 (3): 298.

Metzker, B. (2003). "School Calendars." ERIC Digest. Accessed January 23, 2010. http://www.ericdigests.org/2003-2/calendars.html.

Missouri Department of Health and Senior Services. 2014. "State Seeking Organizations to Serve Meals to Children during Summer Months." Accessed March 1, 2014. http://health.mo.gov/information/news/2014/sfsp21414.

Morgan, L. D. 1929. "How Effective Is Specific Training in Preventing Loss Due to the Summer Vacation?" *Journal of Educational Psychology* 20: 466.

Mraz, M., and T. Rasinski. 2007. "Summer Reading Loss." *Reading Teacher* 60 (8): 784.

Mutchler, S. E. 1993. "Year-Round Education." SEDL Insights on Education. ERIC Document No. 363966.

National Association for Year-Round Education (NAYRE). 2014. "About YRE." Accessed July 1, 2014. http://nayre.org/about.html.

National Center on Education and the Economy. 2007. "Tough Choices or Tough Times." The Report of the New Commission on the Skills of the American Workforce. Accessed April 27, 2013. http://www.ncee.org/wp-content/uploads/2010/04/Executive-Summary.pdf.

National Council For Excellence In Education. 1983. *A Nation at Risk.* Washington, DC: U.S. Department of Education.

National Post. 2013. "Full Comment Forum: Could Canada Cope with a 12-Month School Year?" Accessed July 1, 2014. http://fullcomment.nationalpost.com/2012/05/05/full-comment-forum-could-canada-cope-with-a-12-month-school-year.

Naylor, C. 1995. "Do Year-Round Schools Improve Student Learning? An Annotated Bibliography and Synthesis of the Research." British Columbia Teachers' Federation Research Report. Accessed October 8, 2006. http://www.bctf.bc.ca/ResearchReports/95ei03.

NCLB. 2006. "Legislation, Regulations, Guidance, and Policy for No Child Left Behind." Accessed August 15, 2010. http://www.ed.gov/policy/elsec/leg/esea02/index.html.

Neal, R. 2008. "Extended School Day and Year Are under Review across the Country." *School Reform News,* February 1.

Nelson, M. J. 1928. "How Much Time Is Required in the Fall for Pupils of the Elementary School to reach Again the Spring Level of Achievement?" *Journal of Educational Research* 18: 305.

Neufield, S. 2005. "Year-Round Schooling to End at Coleman Elementary, Officals Say. *Baltimore Sun,* July 28, 2005.

Nevel, J. 2014. "Summer Break Over for Balanced-Calendar Schools." Accessed July 22, 2014. http://www.sj-r.com/article/20140721/NEWS/140729892.

Noonan, M. E. 1926. "Influence of the Summer Vacation on the Abilities of Fifth and Sixth Grade Children." *Contributions to Education* 204: 103.

O'Donnell, P. 2014. "West Side Parents Don't Want School to Start Aug. 13, or Any Move to Year-Round Classes for Their Kids." Cleveland *Plain Dealer,* April 9.

Okanik, B. A. 1994. "The Year-Round College Calendar: Luxury or Necessity?" *Education Canada* 34 (3): 38–41.

Organisation for Economic Cooperation and Development (OECD). *Education at a Glance 2010: OECD Indicators.* Retrieved August 15, 2010, from http://www.oecd. org/document/52/0,3746,en_2649_39263238_45897844_1_1_1_1,00.ht ml

Patterson, M. V. 1925. "The Effect of the Summer Vacation on Children's Mental Ability and on Their Retention of Arithmetic and Reading." *Education* 46: 22.

Pedersen, J. 2012. "The History of School and Summer Vacation," *Journal of Inquiry and Action in Education* 5 (1): 54.

———. 2011. "Length of School Calendars and Student Achievement in High Schools in California, Illinois and Texas." Accessed December 27, 2013. http://scholarship. shu.edu/cgi/viewcontent.cgi?article=2776&context=dissertations.

Pennington, H. 2006. *Expanding Learning Time in High Schools.* Washington, D.C.: Center for American Progress.

Penta, M. 2001. "Comparing Student Performance at Program Magnet, Year-Round Magnet, and Non Magnet Elementary Schools." Raleigh, N.C.: Wake County Public Schools, Department of Evaluation and Research. ERIC Document No. ED457178.

Prendergast, K. A. T. E. Spadlin, and V. J. Palozzi 2007. *Is it Time to Change India's School Year Calendar?* Bloomington, IN: Center for Evaluation and Educational Policy.

Prohm, B., and N. Baenen. 1996. *Are WCPSS Multi-Track Elementary Schools Effective?* Raleigh, NC: Wake County Public School System. ERIC Document Reproduction Service No. ED 395 983.

Rasmussen, K. 2000. "Year-Round Education: Time to Learn, Time to Grow." *Education Update* 42 (2): 1.

Roth, L. 2006. "At Two Facilities with Year-Round Schedule, Academics Improve." Norfolk, VA *Virginian-Pilot*, October 18, B3.

Ryan, J. 2013. "American Schools vs. the World: Expensive, Unequal, Bad at Math." Accessed July 1, 2014. http://www.theatlantic.com/education/archive/2013/12/ american-schools-vs-the-world-expensive-unequal-bad-at-math/281983.

St. Gerard, V. 2007. "Year-Round Schools Look Better All the Time." *Education Digest* 72 (8): 56–58.

Saunders, M. 2006. "Some Kids Ahead of the Classes Never Mind the Thermometer. The State's 'Optional Calendar' Says It's Time for Public Schools to Start." *Omaha World Herald*, July 17, 1.

Scherer, M. 2001. "How and Why Standards Can Improve Student Achievement." *Educational Leadership* 59 (1): 4.

School Holidays Europe. 2014. Accessed December 3, 2013 http://www. schoolholidayseurope.eu.

Schrepel, M., and Laslett. 1936. "On the Loss of Knowledge by Junior High Pupils Over the Summer Vacation." *Journal of Educational Psychology* 27: 299–1936.

Schulte, B. 2009. "Putting the Brakes on 'Summer Slide.'" *Harvard Education Letter* 25: 4.

Serifs, D. 1990. *Year-Round Education: A Closer Look*. Washington, D.C.: U.S. Department of Education, Office of Educational Research and Improvement. Accessed March 2010. ERIC Document No. ED 329008.

Shields, C. M. 1996. "Year-Round Education: Is it Worth the Hassle?" Paper presented at the University of British Columbia Robson Square Lecture Series, Vancouver.

Shields, C. M., and S. L. Oberg. 2000. *Year-Round Schooling: Promises and Pitfalls*. Lanham, MD: Scarecrow.

Silva, E. 2007. *On the Clock: Rethinking the Way Schools Use Time*. Washington D.C.: Education Sector Reports.

Stenvall, M. J. 2001. "Balancing the Calendar for Year-Round Learning." *Principal* 80 (3): 18.

Stoops, T. 2007. "Better Instruction, Not More Time." Raleigh, NC: John Locke Foundation. Texas Education Agency. Accessed August 1, 2010. http://ritter.tea. state.tx.us/perfreport/ci/2009/index.html.

Times Herald. 2014. "More School Districts Look into Year-Round Instruction." Accessed June 1, 2014. http://www.thetimesherald.com/article/20140315/ NEWS01/303150008/More-school-districts-look-into-year-round-instruction?gcheck=1&nclick_check=1.

Trent, S. 2007. "A Descriptive Study of the Effect of Traditional and Year-Round Calendars, Socio-economic Status, and Teacher Tenure Status on Student

Achievement in Two Rural School Systems in Tennessee." Dissertation retrieved from http://digitalcommons.liberty.edu/cgi/viewcontent.cgi?article=1025&conte xt=doctoral.

Ubben, G. C., L. W. Hughes, and C. J. Norris. 2001. *The Principal: Creative Leadership for Effective Schools*, 4th ed. Needham Heights MA: Allyn & Bacon.

U.S. Department of Education. 2010. *NCLB Standards*. Accessed March 1, 2014. http://ed.gov/nclb/landing.jhtml.

Van Mondfrans, A. 1985. "Provo's Year-Round Education Program: First Year Evaluation." Logan, UT: Wasatch Institution for Research and Evaluation. ERIC Document No. 323594.

von Hippel, P. 2007. "Year-Round Schools Don't Boost Learning, Study Finds." Retrieved from http://researchnews.osu.edu/archive/yearrnd.htm.

Weaver, T. 1992. "Year-Round Education: A Strategy for Overcrowded Schools." Washington, D.C.: Office of Educational Research and Improvement. Eric Document No. 342107.

Weiss, J., and R. S. Brown. 2005. "Summer Learning: Research, Policies and Programs." *Teachers College Record* 107 (7): 1429.

———. 2003. "Telling Tales over Time: Constructing and Deconstructing the School Calendar." *Teachers College Record* 105 (9): 1720.

White, W. 1993. "Educational Benefits in Year-Round High Schools." Paper presented at the Annual Meeting of the National Association for Year-Round Education. Las Vegas, NV, February. ERIC Document Reproduction Service No. ED 359 660.

Wildman, L., S. Arambula, D. Bryson, T. Bryson, et al. 1999. "The Effect of Year-Round Schooling on Administrators." *Education* 119: 465–77.

Winters, W. 1994. *A Review of Recent Studies Relating to the Achievement of Students Enrolled in Year-Round Education Programs*. San Diego: National Association for Year-Round Education.

Worthen, B. R, and S. W. Zsiray. 1994. *What Twenty Years of Educational Studies Reveal about Year-Round Education*. Chapel Hill, NC: North Carolina Educational Policy Center.

Ziri, D. 2013. "Israel Cuts School Summer Vacation, Gets US Group Funding for Kids' Program." *Jerusalem Post*. Accessed July 1, 2014. http://www.jpost.com/National-News/Israel-cuts-school-summer-vacation-gets-US-group-funding-for-kids-program-333420.

Zuckerbrod, N. 2007. "Year-Long School Keeps Children Fresh." *Tulsa World*, September, 15.

About the Author

Dr. James Pedersen is currently the principal of South Plainfield High School in South Plainfield, New Jersey, and teaches undergraduate and graduate courses at Felician College and undergraduate courses at Essex County Community College in New Jersey. He has had the opportunity to work in urban and suburban areas as a teacher and administrator and prides himself on the wealth of experiences this has afforded him.

His first book, *The Rise of the Millennial Parents: Parenting Yesterday and Today*, was published in 2013 and is based on current research on parenting styles as well as over two decades of experience as an educator in several school districts across the state of New Jersey. His writing also includes articles on such topics as special education, the importance of college career readiness, parent communication, and calendar reform.

Dr. Pedersen lives with his wife, Faith, and their three children, Emily, Veronica, and Cynthia.

Contact Me

I value the insights and experiences of my readers and enjoy the exchange of ideas.

Please contact me with questions, comments, concerns, or any kind of feedback regarding the material contained here. I appreciate your thoughts and the opportunity to further engage in the exciting topic of how year-round education should be implemented throughout the nation's schools.

You can contact me via e-mail at jamesmpedersen1@gmail.com or follow me on Twitter @jpedersen1.

I hope that you have found this book informative, useful, and instructional. I wish to hear your thoughts and opinions so that discourse regarding this subject continues and moves forward until the masses fully realize the importance of having a complete and balanced education that more closely resembles the rest of society that functions on a twelve-month calendar.